Metaphors of
FAITH

WORDS OF A PRAYING WOMAN

by Mrs. Patsy Bazile

Omniversal Publishing House
5510 Greenwich Drive
Arlington, TX 76018

Copyright © 2015 by Patsy Bazile and Moksha-Media.com, Daymond E. Lavine
Cover Design by Moksha Media.com, Daymond E. Lavine
All rights reserved. No part of this book may be reproduced or transmitted in any form or by any means without written permission from the author.

10 9 8 7 6 5 4 3 2 1

Library of Congress Control Number: 2015917135
ISBN 978-0-9961323-0-5

Without limiting the rights under copyrights reserved above, no part of this publication may be reproduced, stored in or introduced into a retrieval system, or transmitted, in any form or by any means (electronic, mechanical, photocopying, scanning, video presentation, audio recording, or otherwise), without the prior written permission of both the copyright owners and the above publisher of this book.

For additional information about the author, to book a signing event, or for information on acquiring written permission in the case of brief quotations embodied in critical articles, interviews and reviews, visit www.patsybazile.com.

by Mrs. Patsy Bazile

Dedications

This book is dedicated to and in loving memory of my precious Mother, Mrs. Helen Watkins Espree-Jones.

She has graciously left fingerprints of love on my heart, and they will remain there forever as reminders of a legacy of her guiding principles. She has instilled in me morals, values, faith, and love for what she taught me is "a Higher Power whose love is greater than all others." Her teachings serve as strongholds on my spirit to maintain faith that is unwavering and trust in the Lord—my God Almighty, my Alpha and Omega—that is unbreakable!

This book is also dedicated to my only son and most precious gift from God, Daymond Eli Lavine.

There has never been a moment in time at which I have not felt blessed to have him as my son! I love him more than any words or even tears could ever express. I am so grateful to God for rewarding me and allowing me the honor of being his mother. My son has shown me so much love, respect, and honor in return. And now, as I have been inspired by the Holy Spirit to express the narratives contained in this book under the authority of our Almighty God, my son was called to serve diligently as my editor, graphic designer, typesetter, and publisher! Look at God! Thank you, Lord; and thank you, Son, for your encouragement, support, and your loving inspiration!

I dedicate this book as well to Mr. Dezria Bazile, Jr., my husband and the answer to my prayers…for I know that God has chosen him for me.

My husband and I stick with each other through thick and thin, and I know that the Lord is forever with us! I thank my dear husband for understanding me, even when I disturbed him during late nights or early mornings when the Holy Spirit inspired me to write. Not once did he ever complain. Instead, he supported me in every way. I thank him from the bottom of my heart for all of his support, encouragement, and love for me. I love him, always and forever.

And last but not least, I dedicate this book to my dear friend, Hazel Marie Owens.

How strange it is that we went to high school together, but did not become best friends until we became neighbors years later. God knew just when to make it all happen. As adolescents, we would not have truly understood or appreciated true friendship. So I thank God for His perfect timing! I also thank Him for allowing me to include Hazel as a part of my family, the sister I never had! I thank her for her prayers of blessings, support, and encouragement throughout the writing of this book.

Table of Contents

Prelude 11

Oblivious In Search 19

Care, Where Did You Go? 23

What Would the Lion Do? 27

Gossip…the Hitchhiker 31

Truth or Consequences…What Is Your Delight? 37

Make a U-turn…Blasphemy Ahead! 44

How Big Is Your Mountain? 53

Do We Quibble or Get On Track? 60

Mr. Intimidation and the Wee Mouse 69

Do You Ever Wonder WHY? 83

Zera, Daughter of Faith 92

Author's Purpose

"Ah, so you're writing an a book about God and Christianity. Good! There should be a lot of information that parents and Sunday school teachers can use in their homes and classrooms."

"So you're going to write a book based on your experiences as a school teacher and a Christian. That should be interesting!"

These are a couple of responses that I received once I disclosed to some people that I was in the process of writing a book. However, I was not surprised. I am a retired, certified teacher with 32 years of service. That means my literary inspiration is based on lots of experience.

Before I became a teacher, I worked in the educational system as a paraprofessional. During my paraprofessional years, I encountered many challenges that motivated me to develop a deeper relationship with God. In those moments, I suffered; but now, I am thankful for them. They molded me into the Christian that I am today.

This book does not discuss those challenges of mine, but I can definitely tell you that their undertones are present within my words herein. I am sure that as you read onward, you will be able to figure out many of them for yourself. And, of course, God will assist you as well!

by Mrs. Patsy Bazile

Personally, as the author of this book, I ask only one thing of you. Would you please know and believe that this book is written for the sole purpose of serving as a resource for "Spiritual Outreach." Please understand that I have the very precise motive to help others activate a strong and solid FAITH in God that reveals and destroys every weapon formed against them as children of God! I hope that this book helps you break every chain and every form of bondage that separates you from the love of God and our Savior, Jesus Christ.

In this book, you will learn that much of what you read is supported by scripture. Scripture justifies all of our beliefs in God and His Word. Scripture also helps us to cope with challenges that plague our consciousness with "why?" "how?" and "what can I do?" Scripture helps us to find the answers that we seek. While finding many of those answers, we also find GOD!

I would also like to make this very clear: the contents of this book are for Christians and non-Christians alike. My goal is to capture the attention of anyone...and I do mean ANYONE...with a desire to have God in his or her life! However, the path that God intended for me to use to convey my message orginates from my Christian values.

If you have never asked God for anything, I sincerely hope that you now ask Him to open your heart and your mind to receiving the words contained here in my book. We all need God! I want you to receive every ounce of help and every blessing that Jesus has set aside *just for you*! Stop thinking you are not worthy. Just believe and know that YOU ARE! I speak not from a demanding or offensive place, but rather from a platform for spiritual and religious maturity. I am constantly uplifted by the grace of God. He fills my heart with love and the willfulness to communicate with others about how they can remain positive and successful. While there are many among us who encourage our success and achievements, there are others who doubt us. The devil will sometimes tempt them with a "sneak preview" of what could happen if they try to solicit our failure. When friends and family attempt to defeat us and crush our dreams, it can be traumatic. There could be lasting effects and damages that drive us downhill! But do not sink into hopelessness. If you see that someone has been attacked by deceivers and wrong-doers, become a champion for the grace of God. Come to the rescue of your brother or sister in Christ, my friend! God shall prevail! He deals with deception, and He will surely expose evil and put the devil to shame! I intend for this message to prevail throughout the pages of this book.

I have seen more good days than bad days during my career as a teacher; but during those bad days, God always allowed me to see the silver linings around the gloomy storm clouds. During my bad days, I always found Jesus, and I turned to Him for love and comfort. He met me where I was in order to get me where He wanted me to be. Because of this, my faith has become unbreakable and unyielding. I want you to know that He can, and HE WILL do the very same for you!

I ask that you believe that this book is written with a love that Jesus said we should all have for one another. Allow this love to enter your heart so that you can also touch the lives of others and allow God's light to illuminate your path to salvation. Align yourself with the power of His Will! Because the Holy Spirit has inspired me to "outpour" my faith in the form of literature to help others beyond my immediate reach, I trust that the pages of this book will prove to be a useful resource to you. I pray that it allows you to thrive on God's love throughout various aspects of your life, that is, in your home, on your job, in your school, and even in the House of the Lord!

Before you get started with reading, my friend, know that the prayer that follows is from my heart to yours!

"Lord, hear the cry of my sisters and brothers right now! These are Your Children and they are in need of you! As I intercede on their behalves, I'm asking You, Lord, and in the name of Jesus, please to ERASE all doubts that have ever existed in their minds regarding your connection and infinite love for them! FORGIVE AND BLOCK OUT every negative observation or judgment they have developed concerning anything and anybody because they were blinded by the devil's deceptive tactics! Break every chain of captivity and loosen all bondage that has denied them the privilege to experience a joy that can only be found in You, our true God of Justice! Let there be restoration, healing, deliverance, and financial blessings as only You can provide for them, in your name, which is only the best for them! I ask that their spiritual eyes are opened whereby they will now humble themselves before You. Let them denounce the devil, and denounce all lies. I pray that my brothers and sisters will walk in a manner that is clear for all to see that their footsteps are led by You, our True Master! Dear Lord, please keep them covered by the blood of Jesus and protected with Your armor. May they surrender to Jesus, so that "NO WEAPON FORMED AGAINST THE CHILDREN OF GOD SHALL PROSPER!"

In the Mighty Name of Jesus, Amen!

Enjoy your journey in God's light, my friend! It's your new beginning of a blessed eternity!

by Mrs. Patsy Bazile

Prelude

SERENITY IN PRAYER

We pray to fortify our relationship with God.
We pray because we have faith in His love.
We pray any moment, wherever we may be.
We pray for our blessed SERENITY.

§ § §

S - is for "Stillness," so that we can perceive and accept God's Holy Word.

"Be still and know that I am God"
Psalm 46:10 NKJV

E - is for "Endurance"… during those times of trials and tribulations.

"I will never leave nor forsake you"
Hebrews 13:5 NKJV

R - is for "Restraint," because there are predatory influences that will lure us as prey.

"No weapon formed against you shall prosper"
Isaiah 54:17 NKJV

E - is for "Enlightenment," which invokes conviction, the predecessor of repentance.

> *"Wisdom is the principal thing; therefore get wisdom.*
> *And with all your getting, get understanding."*
> *Proverbs 4:7 NKJV*

N - is for "Never-ending," because our gratitude to God should have no end in exchange for the ultimate sacrifice, His only Son, Jesus!

> *"For God so loved the world that He gave His only begotten Son, that whoever believes in Him should not perish but have everlasting life"*
> *John 3:16 NKJV*

I - is for "Invitation." God loves us all but He gave us "free will" so that we have the liberty to allow Him to dwell in our hearts.

> *"But as many as received Him, to them He gave the right to become children of God, to those who believe in His name"*
> *John 1:12 NKJV*

T - is for "Trust." We must trust in God's grace and glory through the power of our faith.

> *"Trust in the Lord with all your heart, and lean not on your own understanding"*
> *Proverbs 3:5 NKJV*

by Mrs. Patsy Bazile

Y - is for "Yielding," for we must not give in to condoning injustice and partaking in unrighteous deeds.

"For God is not unjust to forget your work and labor of love which you have shown toward His name, in that you have ministered to the saints, and do minister."
Hebrews 6:10 NKJV

WADE THROUGH THE WATERS OF HOPE

Wade through the waters of hope
when things go wrong
and there is no answer.

Wade through the waters of hope
to find the strength
you will need to cope.

Wade through the waters of hope
when the sunshine gives way
to torrential rains.

Wade through the waters of hope
during every peril
and all of your pains.

Life is beautiful; it's a blessing from God.
But no one shall escape
the woes of life's unsettling times.

Jesus loves us so, and may we never forget it.
Else we do fall victim
to inept and false shrines.

by Mrs. Patsy Bazile

Wade through the waters of hope
when your friendship is charred
by another's deception.

Wade through the waters of hope
for your justice is in view
of our Master's perception.

Wade through the waters of hope
when your burden is heavy
and no one seems to care.

Wade through the waters of hope
because He listens throughout
your darkest moments of despair.

Our Lord, Jesus Christ, wept for our sins
but He never promised us
freedom from ups and downs.

God loves us so, still He never agreed
our good deeds would be free
from the scorn of onlooker frowns.

Yet, with God, all things are possible.
Retain your faith, believe, and stay strong!
Wade...just wade...with Him! You'll see.
Sweet times will come...hold on.

Metaphors of Faith: Words of a Praying Woman

THE MEN IN THE WHITE ROBES

In the middle of the night, two men stood,
In the shadows wearing long white robes.
At a distance, staring at me, they stood,
Avoid me not, they did not try to look away.

Besides these men, in this place, there were no others.
Silhouettes in my view, they seemed,
For a moment, I thought they could be brothers.
As they began to appear, and show their detail.

One carried a staff with a wide and curvy handle.
The other held a box trimmed nicely with gems.
Long, grey beards, and on their feet, ancient sandals;
So surreal, like a dream, was any of this real?

From afar, I stood, wondering, "What could that be?"
That box surrounded by light and beaming strands of gold.
"Am I supposed to be here?" I wondered if they would show me.
Was this something that I was supposed to behold?

They nodded their heads, then they moved toward each other.
This moment was special, and it was time to begin.
One man stretched his arms outward, his staff raised high.
The box was placed on a pillow, for what was to come then.

by Mrs. Patsy Bazile

They began to step back, nodding to each other again,
Leaving the gift behind, beckoning from the tall thick grass.
The bearded men were gone in seconds, no trace of them.
But the gift shined so brightly, even then, without them.

I was six years of age, but it would all become clear,
What this experience had meant, this vision God had shown.
Those men, God-sent, and that gift was for me.
I tell God each day, "Thank You," as he smiles on His throne.

The poem above was written as a true recollection of a vision that I experienced at the age of six. Jesus reveals Himself to us according to our level of understanding. Acknowledge your visions and dreams, and those of your children as well. It is our duty to encourage ALL that is of God!

ASK HIM

It matters not who you are;
you are a child of God.
It matters not where you are;
you are a child of God.

It matters not the wrong you've done;
you are a child of God.
It matters not your past, how dark;
just give your all to God!

For whom among us is determined to be perfect?
His Word is clear and tells us…no one!"
Though we stumble in life, or even fall;
His promise is that He will forsake no one.

It's never too soon or too late
to call on our Lord, King Jesus.
His love is great and patient! Move on.
Keep your faith, believe, you must.

It matters not, oh no, indeed,
what others say or do to you.
Pray and ask that Jesus knows
what is in your heart is pure and true…

by Mrs. Patsy Bazile

Oblivious In Search

Oblivious…this is a word defined as "lacking of knowledge; unmindful; forgetful." Its definition is a concatenation of undesirable adjectives describing the mental state of an individual, or a given set of individuals.

My thoughts became flooded in the stillness of one early dawn as I visualized a person of no particular race, creed, or color—completely mysterious. This person was deficient of any identity at all…one that was neither male or female, just there. But then, the vision in my mind expanded and gave way to a myriad of people of variable ages, those ranging from newborns beaming with new life, to the old and feeble dimmed by their burdening pasts. Then a strange revelation became apparent to me! The babies and the adolescents were jovial, conducting themselves in ways typical of children. They laughed, frolicked, and jumped about. However, those who were beyond their youthful years or nearing the end of their earthly lives exhibited confusion, devastation, and even internalized pain and hurt. I could see all of this as I hovered above every one of them. I was completely aware of them; yet, they seemed to not notice me at all! So, I questioned in my mind, "Who are these people?" and "Why am I seeing this and hearing the conversations among them?" Unexpectedly, I received a response. A distinctive voice from afar replied, "They are many, but excluding the very young, all answer to the same name…

Oblivious." Curiously, I questioned again, "What justifies this state of existence?"

I listened for more of the explanation...

There was no response. Instead, the very words that formed the answer to my question scrolled before my eyes! They read, "Their full name is, in fact, 'Oblivious In Search' for they wander by night and day; lost, unaware in despair, confused, and unmindful in their present state."

In an instant, the vision was gone. But the impression was long-lasting. An urge within me led to the reading of the Holy Word. I was guided to 1 Corinthians 13:11 NKJV, which offers, "When I was a child, I spoke as a child, I understood as a child, I thought as a child; but when I became a man, I put away childish things."

A sigh of relief...for my vision was made crystal clear!

The loaded term "man" in the Bible verse of 1 Corinthians 13 accounted for all of "mankind." In my vision, the children all possessed individual names because they were young, innocent, and fully present in their moments of bliss, unable to maturely distinguish right from wrong. For this reason, they were protected by the Higher Power!

by Mrs. Patsy Bazile

I pondered upon my vision even harder: I remembered hearing conversations spoken among the teenagers and the older adults. I could sense the spiritual connections bonding them all. The teens shared stories of how—despite their desires to show love and respect for their parents, do well in school, and make good of themselves—they still made bad choices, all because of the "glittering deceptions" of Satan. They had become fatigued by incessant teasing and torment inflicted by their so-called friends. They had also been labeled "crazy" at the slightest sign of praise for and acceptance by someone called "Jesus Christ." The adults expressed different points of view, and their stories were confessional in nature. Many had difficulty remembering their younger years, but those who could reminisce with precise recollection recalled the joyful times in their lives. They once loved the Lord; and, early on, they had been diligent in serving Him as Christians. Yet, when life threw them a "curve ball," they let devastating events lead to their loss of hope. These now former Christians had become examples of how Satan plays his games! Withered and wearily aged, the adults demonstrated the effects of Satan's seduction showcased by illusions of better lives in his realm of the world. Because they had given Satan full access to their minds, he claimed residency in their hearts. Sadly, they had allowed Jesus to be forced out…

1 Corinthians 3:16-17 NKJV tells us, "Do you not know that you are the temple of God and that the Spirit of God dwells in you? If anyone defiles the *temple* of God, God will destroy him. For the temple of God is holy, which *temple* you are."

As Christians, we must pray for those who are falling by the wayside! We must partake in the challenge of piercing the minds of the *Oblivious*. We must inspire hope and the willfulness of all to confess their sins to God. And we must illustrate the allowance of God to dwell within our beings. The King of the Universe, within and without, is willing to help us and teach us. He is a Lord of Forgiveness so that all, including those who were once named Oblivious, may enter again into His loving Kingdom of Grace and Mercy, again and forever more. Yet, I do caution: we are all human and despite our wishes to adhere to the teachings of Jesus, dealing with the Oblivious can prove to be challenging. Do not fret! Hold on to God's unchanging hand. Help the Oblivious. Stay strong in your discernment when determining the ills of them. And do not walk away…

Say a prayer for the Oblivious upon your acquaintance with them. Then, lovingly acknowledge your blessed task:

Thank you, O Lord, for my recognition of they who answer to the name Oblivious. I intercede on their behalf in the name of your son, Jesus, that they instead be renamed Unbound, free from any and all sources of evil; and that all saving grace and mercy is let loose upon them, bringing them back into the family of Christ, and setting them free to roam the earth no longer as…

Oblivious…in search.

Amen!

by Mrs. Patsy Bazile

Care, Where Did You Go?

I had a little chat with my cares today. I jotted several down, and I began to speak to them. Some of them were big, some of them...not so much. But each was unique. And every care required special needs.

The more I chatted, the more my attention focused on the times I had prayed. I thought about how I addressed all of my cares, the mass of them spanning many different areas of my life; yet, I directed my prayers at the single true source of all, He who loves and protects us.

As believers in God, we possess "faith." But sometimes, we fail to notice when our faith has fallen under attack." For many, all hope is lost when things do not go well. And this is when our cares become "problems" that seem to linger on and on.

DO NOT BLAME GOD! Take hold of yourself! He is with you every step of the way...just as He has promised.

Though your cares are still there, still hanging around, tugging at your soul and cramping your style, be mindful of the prayers that you deliver! Most importantly, take responsibility for guiding them to where they must go.

I challenge you to ask questions to your cares, just as I did; they will respond. I questioned. I listened. And for me…here is what my cares had to say:

"Care, why don't you go?" I asked.

A single care responded, "I know you prayed to 'forgive,' but 'not forgiving' seems so much easier for you. I simply stayed right here!"

"Care, why don't you go?" I asked again.

Then another care responded, "I know you prayed to 'love,' but to 'hate' seems much more powerful to you. I decided to tarry too!"

Once more, in a bold and clear voice, I questioned, "Care, why don't you go!"

Behold the voice of yet another care responded, "I know you prayed for the removal of 'jealousy,' but my sticking around creates a false, but lovely euphoric reaction. The longer I stay, the more I offer. So I loaf around here as well!"

The response of each care painted a clear picture for me! I understood why they had not reached the destination I intended for

them. It was simple: the faith on which they were meant to travel had *fallen under attack*.

Think of a time when you were headed in one direction, but you got distracted by something "shiny" but not so good. Think of how you lost focus on your goal and could no longer figure out how you might arrive at your planned destination. If this has never happened to you, then you should shout, "Praise the Lord!" But if you have experienced this or you are going through it right now, please take heed to the message that I am about to convey to you.

When we ask God for blessings and direct our cares to Him, we must think to take authority over all evil influences and enemies in advance of doing so. We must bind them up in the name of Jesus, for they will cause our cares to take a wrong turn, venture down unknown paths, be hindered and halted in progress, or sadly, remain idle at the source, thus…leaving us to wallow in lazy attempts to make things easier for ourselves. Christians, the enemies of our faith act as the dishonorable soldiers of Satan. They stand guard, ever ready to intercept the promises that God has already made to His children and "royal heirs" to His Kingdom.

During your pursuit to conquer the enemies of your faith, remain steadfast and immovable in your prayers, wearing the whole of the armor of God. Fearlessly wear it and conquer those iron clad by none other than the "Prince of Darkness." Speak to your cares today! Allow them to reveal what lead them astray.

My prayer for all readers of this message follows:

By the power of the Holy Spirit, you are now in possession of a "renewed faith" that has authority over all evil influences, making room only for what is of God! Thus, you are now able to direct ALL cares to only Jesus Christ, as our intercessor, and unto His Father in Heaven, God above!

by Mrs. Patsy Bazile

What Would the Lion Do?

The lion has made its claim to fame by being known as the "King of the Jungle." It has a mighty roar, a proud and non-fearing strut, and is always in constant search of prey. The lion is well aware of the fear it instills in other beasts of the wild, and it dares not lose face among its own kind!

Once captured, its prey is doomed, for upon the weak, the lion shows no mercy. It roams the land merely for self-gain. The theory of survival of the fittest justifies the lion's existence, while characteristics crucial to the lion's vitality are revealed to man through scientific studies of animal behavior.

But what if?

What if the lion suddenly came face to face with Jesus in the jungle! Thinking outside the box, I see that same mighty, fearsome, and ferocious king of the wild stopping dead in its tracks! It wonders in silence, "Is this the presence of a higher power?" Then Jesus would say to it, "Lion, enough! Be still, for I have come to change that which you once called your world." The lion's perception of reality would then befall into absolute amazement, for a revelation would confirm that it is now in the in the company of the true "Master of All Things." And at the sound of the voice of Jesus, the lion would yield to the "King of Kings."

Oh, what an astonishing transformation! The lion is no longer one with a mighty roar, but a kitten with a soft, timid purr. It is now unaware of its title, losing face and forgetting concern for only itself. It realizes that its walk is no longer proud and bold; but, weak and uncertain. And internally, the lion then poses several questions:

"Am I now the prey?"

"Why am I so fearful?"

"Why do I now feel the need for protection?"

Although the lion knows the answers to these questions, it still looks up to Jesus for affirmation. Jesus already knows the thoughts of the lion, yet He still allows the lion to approach, pleading, "Teach me Your way, O Lord. I will walk in Your truth. May my heart fear Your name" Psalms 86:11 NLV. Hence, Jesus responds, "I am the way, the truth, and the life. No one comes to the father except through me." Now if this is the response of Jesus to the transformed lion, isn't it imperative that we examine ourselves as Christians, our spiritual walk, and the real messages we convey, whether we be leaders for or followers of Christ?"

by Mrs. Patsy Bazile

I believe that once we receive Jesus as our personal Savior, we must keep our hearts open so that He may abide within us. I have seen signs that read, "Jesus is my Co-Pilot," but I would rather one that reads, "Jesus is my *Pilot*." Over time, my spiritual growth has instilled in me the belief that Jesus, the head of my life, is the Pilot that guides me as His vessel to "getting the job done!" I state this for the sole purpose of self-justification, and not *self-gain*.

All too often, God will give us instructions throughout various aspects of our daily lives. He will speak to us at our jobs, our homes, during our travels, and even within our ministries. And we will listen to Him. We will try to abide by his commands, but even then, we will sometimes notice that the good times begin to fade. While the blessings may be rolling in, we will decide to get beside ourselves by boasting, bantering, and carrying on. And that is when our lives will still start to unravel: the result of an "inflated ego" that has given way to "blind revision." As Christians, we must allow God to work through us; this is not to be misunderstood as *us working through Him*. What a common mistake this is because many of us simply forget that He does not need us…

Our Lord God is the creator! In all that we do, we must do so in faith and by the command of none other than the Holy Spirit. We must glorify God and give Him the highest praise! We must also take heed to his nurturing care as He who blesses us with the wonderful gifts of "wisdom" and "discernment." Let us remember that as children of the King, we are all created for a distinct purpose... one that should not be abused, hindered, plagued, or discredited by anyone!

In our everyday lives, as well as in our ministries, God wants us to illustrate Christ-like behaviors that invoke a desire for others to come into the family of Christ. Though the lion still holds its title among beasts, and as its character remains admired by many, we should take heed to a discovery seen through the vision of our "spiritual eye." The lion is and will always be conquerable. *This is the will of God.* There are several scriptures that support this truth. My personal favorite—the one that helps me deal with the many enemies or forces that try to hinder my faith and action for doing those things which are pleasing to God—is found in this scripture:

> *"who through faith, subdued kingdoms, wrought righteousness, obtained blessings, stopped the mouths of the lions"*
> *Hebrews 11:33 NKJV*

by Mrs. Patsy Bazile

Gossip...the Hitchhiker

Gossip is a hitchhiker! It wants to tag along with anyone, anywhere, at anytime it has the opportunity to do so. Gossip is always looking for a place to hang out, and it is sad to say that gossip is a permanent resident in many of our homes. Even though it may have its very own seat at the kitchen table, it likes to get out too. It will follow us from home to our workplaces, to our schools, and even into the grocery stores. Everywhere! Yet, Gossip still has a "special place" it particularly likes to visit. If anyone volunteers to give it a ride, it is sure to pop up in the House of God!

Be not deceived, for Gossip is not ignorant! It knows that God has not made provisions for it anywhere, especially in the church. The Bible tells us that "a perverse man stirs up dissension, and a gossip separates close friends" (Proverbs 16:28 NIV). So how is it that Gossip so easily slips into our churches? Well, here is the simple answer to what may initially seem like a perplexing question: Gossip is a loiterer!

Well before church services begin, Gossip tends to arrive early. It tarries outside, initially starting out with simple chit chat, like "How is your morning, Sister So-and-so?" and "Nice weather, we're having, Brother So-and-So. Don't you think?" But then, it latches on to someone, and it strides on in through the doors of the House of the Lord. It beckons, "Come on in. You're going my way! Why not continue our conversation in the comfort of a pew?" Just like that, a Christian falls victim to becoming an instrument of Gossip! Then Gossip becomes all too thankful to use this Christian as a tool to fulfill its purpose. It wants everyone to know of its relationship with a child of God; yet, what it has to offer in return is not a fair trade. Its token of appreciation is only a new alias for the Christian. Christian becomes Gossiper; and then, Gossip begins to revel in creating reckless and ill-informed commentary. Meanwhile, Mr. or Ms. Gossiper serves as the mouthpiece of the deceiver!

Gossip is cunning. It knows that many of us are weak. In moments of weakness when we doubt God's Word, Gossip makes all attempts to make a stand. It shouts out half-truths on a self-proclaimed pedestal of knowledge, and it strives to prove its existence among the Lord's most faithful! At the same time, Gossip attempts to play mind games with us. For example, it might encourage the twisting of Biblical verses, quoting words such as "for all have sinned and fall short of the glory of God," (Romans 3:23 NKJV) while forgetting to mention "being justified freely by His grace through the redemption that is in Christ Jesus," (Romans 3:24 NKJV).

Once within the walls of our holy sanctuaries, Gossip strives to remain relevant. Scanning among the fold, it seeks to affirm those who are weak and to tempt others who cannot recognize it. When Gossip finds those it can entice, it whispers hidden secrets or shameful details about others to them. This is what Gossip thrives on, for it wishes to distract us from learning a secret about itself. In actuality, Gossip is weak. In the face of those who are strong, Gossip deteriorates because it is insecure. Shrouding itself in deceitful cloaks to hide its low self-esteem, Gossip builds networks of supportive allies with mutual characteristics. And these dysfunctional networks haphazardly swell by trying to make others look bad, thus seeking to virally spread distorted proclamations anywhere it can.

Gossip speaks of the faults or failings that it has found in others. It cannot be trusted because it is incapable of "keeping uncovered secrets." Once juicy bits of information become available, Gossip cannot wait to repeat them without the trustees' consent or knowledge. In doing so, it holds tight to its camouflage, trying to protect itself when it says things like, "…but, I really meant you no harm" or "I thought you wouldn't mind." Still, some people see right through this. When Gossip is exposed, it becomes uncomfortable. Those who are strong in the name of Christ see it for what it really is. The strongest Christians know that Gossip's true intent is to hurt others; and so, they bring Gossip to a halt, catching it red-handed in a lie!

When Gossip can no longer hide, it realizes that misconceptions about it have given way to its true nature—for example, the truth that gossip does not limit itself only to an assembly of women. No! Gossip has been around since the days of old when the widows of 1 Timothy 5:13 NKJV wandered as "gossips and busybodies, saying things they ought not to." The Bible further states that "He who is devoid of wisdom despises his neighbor, but a man of understanding holds his peace" (Proverbs 11:12 NKJV) and "A gossip betrays a confidence, but a trustworthy person keeps a secret." (Proverbs 11:13 NIV). To elaborate, Proverbs 20:19 NIV warns, "A gossip betrays a confidence; so avoid anyone who talks too much." Gossip is not prejudiced. Remember, it will accept a ride from anyone, *even you*!

Don't allow Gossip to bamboozle you. It can only bring you harm whether you are its target or its "friend." Do not blind yourself to its destructive potential. It is not a peacemaker, especially in our churches. Those who entertain it do nothing but help it stir up trouble, disrupt the peace, and cause anger and pain among others in fulfillment of its selfish cravings. Gossip criticizes "God's Messenger" instead of focusing on "God's Message." It critiques the singers of the gospel instead of focusing on the teachings of their melodious words. Gossip refuses to accept the task of leading a church ministry, yet it is eager to find faults of the established ministries. Most importantly, Gossip divides us from God by shifting our sights away from the Kingdom of Heaven. Oh, Yes! Gossip is relentless!

Beware! Gossip will not give up easily once it has your attention. But when it does, you must confront it. Search within yourself and take responsibility for the harm that you become capable of inflicting on others. Realize that Gossip is attempting to introduce you to another associate that identifies itself as "the Liar." Alert yourself to their disguises, and listen when they distort the truth and denounce your identification of their disobedience to the teachings of Christ. Stay strong when they respond by trying to justify their actions, for Proverbs 18:7-8 NIV says, "The mouths of fools are their undoing, and their lips are a snare to their very lives. The words of a gossip are like choice morsels; they go down to the inmost parts." As Christians, we have the obligation to refrain from causing turmoil in the lives of our brothers and sisters in faith. It is a blessing when we have grown in our spiritual presence on Earth. Remember, God smiles on us when we recognize that "those who guard their mouths and their tongues keep themselves from calamity" (Proverbs 21:23 NIV).

Dear reader, keep in mind that recognizing the "gossiper" does not imply misconduct of ourselves while we offer the teachings of Jesus Christ. We should not condone the actions of the gossiper or the liar, and we are not obligated to remain in the company of them. However, we must pray for them! This may be a difficult task to accomplish, but reflect on your humanity. Think back to those moments in your life when you have acted in ways that were not pleasing to God. Undoubtedly, someone prayed for you! Someone appealed to Jesus on your behalf, while you may never know just how much they concerned themselves with your misfortunes. When we pray for those who need it most, we free ourselves from all pride and partiality. We permit ourselves to offer sincerity in prayer for others, asking God to bring them to a place of surrender and confession of their sins. We allow ourselves to kneel to God, and with a pure heart we ask that our brothers and sisters are unclenched from Gossip's tight grips, because their malicious engagements are not pleasing in His sight.

When we allow God to live within our hearts, He helps us remain righteous. Sure, there are times when we stumble or even fall, but we rise again! God is there to support us just as He has promised! Follow the teachings of the Holy Bible, and do not make room for Gossip! Pass it up. Bind it up in the name of Jesus each time it tries to nudge your shoulder. When it whispers in your ear, deny it. Gossip is not worthy of entering the House of the Lord.

When I was young, someone told me, "We should keep our mouths shut until it is time or necessary to speak." As a child, I did not realize just how important these words were, but now it's a different story! I listen to Lord who fills my heart. May you let Him fill your minds and fuel your love for your brothers and sisters as well. You may find yourself heeding the strength of those words as well! Amen!

by Mrs. Patsy Bazile

Truth or Consequences... What Is Your Delight?

Do you believe in God? Do you believe that He gave His only Son, Jesus Christ, to deliver us from evil and cleanse us of our sins? Do you believe that God offered Himself to the world in the form of flesh, suffering and daggling in pain and agony, from nails on a rugged cross? And do you also believe that had Jesus Christ—the physical embodiment of God on Earth—cried out, "Father, save me!" then it would have been so? I am confident in saying that most of us would say, "Yes." But consider this: what would have been the effect of Jesus choosing to retain His life here on Earth in abandonment of the children of God?

Today, we are blessed to know that God loves us, despite the imperfection inherent to our being. Jesus shed his blood for us to allow us the chance to become "perfect" in the wholeness of God! "But this Man [Jesus Christ], after He had offered one sacrifice for sins forever, sat down at the right hand of God, from that time waiting till His enemies are made His footstool. For by one offering He has perfected forever those who are being sanctified" (Hebrews 10:12-14 NKJV). Only by that single offering, did Jesus Christ set into motion the actions necessary to allow humanity the opportunity to be purified and cleansed of their sins. Even the death of Christ was perfect, and the Bible tells us "…we have been sanctified through the offering of the body of Jesus Christ once for *all*" (Hebrews 10:10 NKJV). Had Jesus not died, there would be no "grace and truth" (John 1:17 NKJV).

A world without grace…can you fathom such a concept? In studying the Bible, we come to realize that the only way we can be validated in the glory of God is by His grace! No man, alone in his accomplishments, has ever mastered the "sufficient and perfect" adherence to all universal laws. Romans 3:23 NKJV reminds us of this when we read, "for all have sinned and fall short of the glory of God." It is Jesus, the Son of God, who came, died for us, and rose again to validate our redemption. But what does that really mean for us? Let us think deeper. If Jesus had not perished on the cross on our behalves, then what would have happened to love? How could we know of faith and prayer? Would there have been a place called "church"? And, Oh my Lord! Access to the Kingdom of God, how could we even have come to know of it?

Simply put, as for the Glory of God and His magnificence, we would have no connection to it. Love, one of the most precious extensions of God's grace, would be insignificant to us. But because Christ died in our honor and God "loved" us so much that He bestowed His son on Earth among men, we know of love. We have a profound and keen sensibility regarding love. Most importantly, we know *how* to love. Yet, let's face it: as Christians, we sometimes have a hard time offering our special testimony of demonstrating our Christ-like love for all people. We live in a society filled with people who possess various characteristics, ways of thinking, and ways of doing things. All of humanity is complex, and it is our complexities that cause great tensions among us in a world that we must learn to share and cohabitate in. But let's keep it real! Christians are tested. Many of us can attest that at least once in our lives, someone has gotten on our "last nerves." "Lord, help me, Sweet Jesus!" Can you remember saying something like this at some point in your life when someone may have vexed you? "Come on and help me, right now, Oh Lord, because my love is being tested!" Sounds familiar, Christian? Amen, and have a laugh right now if you must!

If you have not realized it yet, take notice of the fact that many people mistakenly link positive thinking to the Christian faith. But I would like point out an undeniable distinction. People who elect to think positively about the decisions or situations at hand in their lives are simply choosing to "block out" all elements that are negative according to their thoughts. They worry about not experiencing the outcome that they are hoping to create or influence. So ignoring negativity allows these people to obtain the self-confidence they need to propel them to move forward toward meeting their goals.

Picture a student in gym class. Today, this student will be trying to climb the rope for the very first time. He is full of fear and anxiety. Those around him may not notice it, but he trembles, and he does not want to endure the humiliation and teasing that will come from his peers if he fails to climb that rope. Then, a voice begins to speak to him from deep within his soul. This voice emanates from something much bigger than himself. The voice encourages him. "You can do this!" it speaks. "You are young, energetic, strong, and healthy! You can do this!" the voice confirms. The student then feels a gentle force behind him that nudges him forward. Subsequently, when the student finally takes to the rope, he relinquishes all of his fear! He climbs that rope and ascends higher and higher. There is no longer anything for him to worry about. In fact, there never really was anything to fear because that student was already determined to succeed! So is that all it really took?

Do not be mistaken, dear reader. The Christian faith is not grounded in our own "self-assurance"—the blind and pompous act of wrapping ourselves in the notion that only we are the centers of our faith. It is Jesus who centers our faith! And even religion itself cannot overshadow this truth. Our faith in God is made possible by the blood of CHRIST! It is Jesus through whom God has "spoken to us" (Hebrews 1:2 NKJV) so that we could know that "faith is the substance of things hoped for, the evidence of things not seen. (Hebrews 11:1 NKJV). Now that we are able to accept God into our hearts, we can be certain that He will speak to us in our times of both joy and sadness. He will welcome us to the family as co-heirs to His Kingdom with our Lord and Savior, Jesus Christ!

Yet…what is faith without prayer? Who would we pray to if Jesus had not been crucified for our salvation? How would we know of "God who art in Heaven"? Our existence would be devoid of knowing about the ultimate act of "perfect" love. There would be no perfect sacrifice. And we would not know of the personal relationships that Jesus has encouraged us to have with God for ourselves. Yes, today, we can be thankful that there is no excuse for not "praying" so that we might experience the grace of God.

Oh, dear reader, there would not even be a church today! Obviously, the physical house of Christ would not exist, but that is not all. We would not even be able to relate to one another in adherence with the teachings of Christ. "Now you are the body of Christ, and members individually. And God has appointed these in the church: first apostles, second prophets, third teachers, after that miracles, then gifts of healings, helps, administrations, varieties of tongues." 1 Corinthians 12:27-28 NJKV tells us. How could we have ever come to follow Christ with these appointments in the name of the Lord so that we could appeal to our Almighty Heavenly Father?

The death of Jesus Christ was profound and far-reaching. My words cannot truly convey just how significant it is for all people who are bonded in the love of Christ. Yet, the concepts that I have pointed out in this testimonial are constructively and carefully conveyed to you by the guidance of my faith and my own internal revelations. My hope is for any reader to utilize my words for the evaluation of his or her own relationship with Jesus. They are written here to be used as faith healers for those who are experiencing some sense of loss, those who live in doubt, those who feel deceived, those who are bereaved, the poor, the rich in earthly gain, the lonely, the sick, and believers as well as non-believers. I say to you—my brother or sister in Christ—that

God loves you whether you love Him or not. Jesus Christ died for us all. However, realize that only when someone welcomes Christ into his or her heart, true joy, blessings, and wonders of "perfect" love emerge.

Reader, always remember that experience of the perfect love of Christ is not free! It requires obedience. I caution you: even the little things to which we give little thought often require obedience. Think of a combination lock. Think of the challenge you face when you try time and time again to twist the dial in ways that you choose to twist it. The lock does not open. But when a voice inside of your head says, "Obey! Use the correct code, and then the lock will open!" and you do as you must, the lock opens. This is an example of the obedience that we must practice when trying to accomplish a goal.

The obedience that we must exercise when accessing the perfect love of Jesus Christ is studying the Holy Word for ourselves. Dig into the Bible for yourself instead of leaving it unused on the bookshelf at home, on the end table in the den or living room, in the drawer of your bedroom night stand, in the back of the pews at church, or even riding in the car with you. This will serve as your "perfect" acknowledgement of obedience to God and the obedience that is required for knowing the love of the Lord. This will also serve as your testimony to knowing the "perfect" obedience that Jesus provided as an example for us study. "Though He was a Son, yet He learned obedience by the things which He suffered" (Hebrews 5:8 NKJV). Be mindful, that Jesus has shown us that obedience is enduring. Think of the words that Paul wrote telling us about Jesus' obedience: "And being found in appearance as a man, He humbled Himself and became obedient to the point of death, even the death of the cross" (Philippians 2:8 NKJV).

Dear reader, in reading my words right now, let free your joy and shout "Hallelujah" in the name of Christ! Always stay committed to His teachings. Exercise the teachings of Colossians 3:12-17 NKJV and "put on love, which is the bond of perfection." Remain steadfast and immovable in your quest to welcome others to know Christ "the vine" in the vineyard of God! Remember that your commitment as a willing servant of the Lord in the House of God is sure to bear fruit in His name (also in John 15:1-8 NKJV).

With a sincere and deeply embedded certainty, I know that there are those who will read this writing of mine—delivered from my soul through the faith and love I have for Christ—and come to appreciate the death of Jesus. They will know just how much it means for mankind. They will come to truly appreciate it, and they will know and accept the truth of the love of Christ. Envisioning the dire consequences of a world without a Lord and Savior who died to save it will be revealed to them just as it was for me. Without a doubt, I know that they will now be able to say and feel the profound implications found in the words, "Yes, Jesus died! For you and for me! He died for ALL of us! And for this we shall delight in the glory of God!"

Make a U-turn... Blasphemy Ahead!

"Blasphemy," as defined by miriam-webster.com, is "the act of insulting or showing contempt or lack of reverence to God." If we only pay attention of the portion of this definition regarding "insulting, showing contempt, and lacking reverence," then the word may seem unimportant. However, it is the portion of the definition for blasphemy that states "to God" that makes us want to pay closer attention to it.

Those of us who are deeply grounded in our Christian faith believe that God is the Supreme and Infinite Master of the Universe. We have accepted God in our lives as the perfect and all-powerful Spirit whose essence is interwoven into our daily lives. We have further responded to his invitation to dwell in our hearts and guide our souls. We trust and know that God is there for us all of the time. We also know that His grace and power over all that exists is good all of the time. God's love for us is infinitely larger than any problems we have now or ever will have!

An exhibition of the presence of God in many of our churches involves members of the congregations "being touched by the Holy Spirit," or as some Christians say, the "Holy Ghost." Regardless of the name used, God's presence is "highly praised!" I know that you may have doubt in your heart that makes you question, "Is this Holy Spirit considered divine?" However, I must answer, "You better believe it!" I will repeat, "The Holy Spirit is highly praised!"

Sometimes during many of our church services, the Spirit becomes so intense and pervading that the atmosphere turns intoxicating! I could not make a statement like this without having experienced it for myself! There are times in the House of the Lord when the Spirit steps in and takes full control. Everyone begins to clap, jump, or shout while giving glorious praises to God! Others run and fall to their knees to thank Him! Meanwhile, some folks receive the gift of speaking in tongues right there on the spot! But, dear reader, The Holy Spirit does not interact with everyone in the same way, so let me make this perfectly clear: If you see someone who is just sitting there, appearing to refuse to demonstrate any of the previously mentioned actions, do not judge this person! The "state of meditation" is real as well, and some people simply become more focused on the Word of God during moments of sheer joy and excitement. They seek and find clarity while they witness the awesomeness of the Lord! Thus, it is not for those around this person to know where God has met him or her. In those moments of meditation, God keeps his pupil right there where he wants him or her to be. And remember, He hears even the faintest cries from those who seem to be the most quiet of us all!

Now that I have addressed God's presence amongst us, and the exhibition of His power and control during moments of praise and glory, I have a few questions for you:

(A) If you have not experienced being touched by the Holy Spirit, but have witnessed it through others, how should you react to this?

(B) When you react—that is, if you react—then how do you determine if your actions are positive, negative, or even acceptable?

(C) If you discover that your reaction was negative or unacceptable, then how do you respond? What are the consequences for this reaction?

Question 1: How should you react to those touched by the Holy Spirit, since I haven't been?

Even though you have only served as a witness to others being touched by the Holy Spirit, the last thing you want to do is make it easy for the devil to single you out. Do not allow him to call you friend and name you "Mocker"! It is imperative that you truly understand what mockery is. The Bible describes mockery as a form of hypocritical behavior worthy of God's protection against it: "With hypocritical mockers in feasts, they gnashed upon me with their teeth. Lord, how long wilt thou look on? Rescue my soul from their destructions, my darling from the lions" (Psalms 35: 15-17 KJV).

Examples of hypocrites are those who ridicule shouters and shakers in the House of God, while the Holy Spirit may be stepping in and bringing uncontrollable joy to his loyal children. Laughing, making jokes, and saying hurtful things to people who "demonstrate" their faith is dangerous! In fact, these actions are downright despicable, and they are also self-destructive to the perpetrators. So now you might question why I say this? Well the Bible tells us so. Mockery of the genuine actions of God's children in response to his awesome power is blasphemy against the Holy Spirit! Blasphemy grieves the Lord and will not be tolerated by Him. In 2 Chronicles 36:16 KJV, the Bible tells us "But they mocked the messengers of God, and despised his words, and misused his prophets, until the wrath of the Lord arose against his people, till there was no remedy." Mark 3:29 (NIV) elaborates, "Whoever blasphemes against the Holy Spirit will never be forgotten, they are guilty of eternal sin." In many cases, the mocker's primary downfall is envy. He or she may not have a solid relationship with God; thus, looking at someone basking in God's awesome and graceful allure becomes intimidating to this person. In other cases, people may be guilty of sloth. They are lazy with regard to their spiritual growth and maturity. Thus, when they witness the actions of others who have become strongly connected to God, they choose simple and frivolous responses such as laughing and poking fun at them.

Question 2: How do you know if your responses to those touched by the Lord are positive, negative, or acceptable?

Based on my answer to Question 1, you more than likely know how to answer Question 2. Essentially, any actions that involve ridiculing, imitating, making jokes about, or saying hurtful things about jovial praise-givers in the church are negative. These actions are blasphemous! In fact, they are ABSOLUTELY UNACCEPTABLE. Let us ponder this realization for a moment, and let us think about the purposes for which we go to the House of the Lord. If our minds are clouded and our hearts are poisoned, how will we learn more about God and His will for us? We will be unable to obey Him and glorify Him. Then, the mockers will emerge from those who become wayward in the House of God. They will blaspheme in feeble attempts to corrupt and hurt those around them. And this will occur because these blasphemers have not opened their minds and hearts to ask God to dwell within them.

If the mocker does not ask God for forgiveness, then misfortune and misery will always follow. Mockery is a punishable state of denial by the Almighty Creator. Reference Mark 3:29 (KJV) again. Mockers suffer the cycle of despicable contemptuous pleasure followed by internalized misery and self-loathing. Only when the mocker chooses to break this cycle will God approve of his or her actions! Thanking God for touching his children in the House of Praise and Worship is pleasing to Him! You must enter the doors of your church with good intentions at all times, especially when God is filling the place with His grace and invigorating presence. Responding in this manner is perhaps the perfect way to walk in the light of God while bearing witness to those being touched by Him.

by Mrs. Patsy Bazile

Question 3: What are the consequences for mocking God?

Let us study two verses in Chapter 3 of the book of Mark:

Verily I say unto you, All sins shall be forgiven unto the sons of men, and blasphemies wherewith soever they shall blaspheme: But he that shall blaspheme against the Holy Ghost hath never forgiveness, but is in danger of eternal damnation. (Mark 3: 28-29 KJV)

Dear reader, blasphemy is not pardonable by God! It is vital that you also know this. For this reason, I am compelled to further elaborate on others ways we might mock the Lord. By all means, do not risk losing God's love as a result of mocking, and ultimately blaspheming, against our Lord and Savior…

Repentance without forsaking and restitution…

Many of us have grown spiritually and have gotten to a point in our lives where we do not have a problem with confessing our sins. We confess because we know that Romans 3:23 KJV tell us "for all have sinned and fall short of the glory of God." However, repenting our sins is not where we stop. There is more that we must do!

Sin is defined as a transgression of God's law. But asking for forgiveness when we lie, for example, is not enough. We must forsake telling lies!

Let me further elaborate on this particular case of telling lies. To be more specific, I will extend this example to pertain to someone spreading lies about a fellow church member. Exodus 20:16 (KJV) reads, "Thou shalt not bear false witness against thy neighbour."

Since spreading lies about someone is hurtful and damaging to that person, the liar should make restitution! The liar should go to the person or people who have been hurt and tell them, "I'm sorry." When we confess our sins without repentance, forsaking, and making restitution, we mock the Lord!

Prayer is serious business!

Through prayer, we have the ability to make a spiritual connection with God using our words and our thoughts. In prayer, we give Him thanks for our blessings. In prayer, we ask God to continue to keep us in his grace and to protect our families and general wellbeing. In prayer, we also worship the Lord, and we give to Him our highest praises! Yet, too often, some people treat prayer as if it is merely a tradition, or even worse, a simple habit.

If our prayers are not genuine, then how can we recall what was ever prayed for? Many homes have established a schedule for calling everyone together at a particular time for Bible Study. Then, once that time has passed, they go about their normal lives. However, on the next day, when someone asks questions such as "What chapter and scriptures were discussed," and "What was the moral of the lesson yesterday," many family members offer blank stares. Routines can do this to us!

Even in our churches, routines can ruin our intentions for genuine prayer. Sad but true, as time progresses, prayer meetings that are called in many of our churches are converted into choir rehearsals!

A question that might come to your mind is, "How do our prayer meetings ever get diminished?" Well, the reason is that we sometimes forget the purpose of prayer. We must always remember how sacred our ritual of prayer is! None of our conversations with God shall ever be discounted.

The Holy Communion

How many times do we hear people say, "Oh yes, I'm going to church today, it's Communion Sunday!" What exactly do they mean by this? Are they only going to the communion table because it is a matter of how they were raised? Or is it just a custom or a tradition for them? If so, then these folks are missing the point of the Lord's holy supper. They are not partaking in communion to strengthen their bond and their faith in God. And if their connection with God is not strong and sincere, then they might run the risk of partaking in the Lord's Supper with unresolved issues at hand, such as hate, jealousy, and malice that might linger in their hearts.

Let us pray brothers and sisters in Christ that this is not the case!

1 Corinthians 11:27 KJV tells us:

"Wherefore, whosoever eat this bread and drink this cup of the Lord, unworthily, shall be guilty of the body and blood of the Lord" Now we see, that when we partake in the Lord's Supper, and are not worthy, we mock the Lord!"

Make a U-turn!

Wherever you are in your faith, remember that you always have the choice to turn to God for forgiveness and change your trajectory in life. God is always there for us, and whether we choose to acknowledge His power, glory and magnificence, or not, He is and forever will be. We have the opportunity to relish in his splendor, but mocking Him will not get us there. Dear reader, if you have found that by reading this passage, you have partaken in mocking the Lord, MAKE A U-TURN NOW! Do not blaspheme against the Giver of your soul and the Origin of your existence. Marvel at God's wonders. Then let Him reveal your best self as you travel better routes in your new life's journey.

by Mrs. Patsy Bazile

How Big Is Your Mountain?

A mountain...just think about it. It is a large landmass that is much bigger than a hill; and it towers over all of the lands surrounding it. Mountains...they are so large that although there is often a lot to look at and experience all around them, we do not notice any of that, because ...well, they are mountains! They are huge, undeniable marvels in the natural world; thus, it is quite understandable that we often mention "mountains" in our lives as representatives of the problems and difficulties that we endure.

All of the mountains that we climb are different sizes. What we often do not realize is that some of them are there because of us. Throughout our earthly journeys, there are some mountains that we climb because we must prove our faith in God. However, keep in mind that as we toil up and down the sides of some of those mountains, we do so because we have acted in ways contrary to the word of the Lord. God has important assignments for each and every one of us, and when we deviate from His plan and dismiss the work that He has assigned to us, we introduce a brand new "mountain" into our lives.

Mountains...oh, how marvelous they are! In essence, most of those mountains that we face are there because we chose a difficult path to travel in life. Because God knows all, it is not necessary for us to describe our mountains to Him. He already knows the exact dimensions of each one that we labor. We pray, we weep, we beg, and then we toss and turn at night throughout our slumber as a result of our frustration. Some of us may even begin to think that God does not hear us or care for us anymore. But have no fear…for fear is the response of the faithless at a time when they must be most *faithful!*

Beware of losing faith, fellow Christians!

Do not fall victim to the fact that far too often people *only* pray to God for the removal of mountains in their lives. When nothing happens, they become displeased. Their anger with God then becomes a reason for them to disconnect from Him. They make up "stories" about their punishment to justify their mountain not being moved. Yet, the truth is right in front of their very eyes.

I believe that God wants us to look more closely at His Word. There are lessons to be learned from each mountain He has allowed us to endure. Mark 11:23 NKJV states clearly, " For assuredly, I say to you, whoever says to this mountain, 'Be removed and be cast into the sea,' and does not doubt in his heart, but believes that those things he says will be done, he will have whatever he says." It is *our* responsibility, not God's, to speak to our mountains!

Whether we have created our own mountains due to poor decisions, or some other misfortune is the cause, God does not say ignore them. The Bible tells us to speak to the "hill." It will move and "nothing will be impossible for" us (Matthew 17:20 NKJV).

by Mrs. Patsy Bazile

Many people practice fasting and praying to overcome the mountains in their lives. Yet, when they are asked about the true purpose of doing so, they are sometimes hesitant to respond. They do not make the mental connection that these practices are instruments of faith. Some people believe that fasting and praying are the practices that actually *move* mountains in their lives, but this is not so. Prayer and fasting are acts of faith that nourish our souls, our spiritual connections with the Almighty, and our confidence in God's Word. Remember Peter, the disciple who began walking to Jesus on water by faith? It was not until he looked down to the rumbling waters beneath him that he began to sink? He cried out "Lord save me!" And the Lord did. But why did Peter begin to sink? He sank because he became so overwhelmed by his miraculous experience that he allowed his own disbelief to defeat him.

Do not deceive yourself by thinking that God is moved by our acts of fasting and praying. We do not possess the authority to move Him! However, through prayer and fasting, our flesh is forced to submit to our "spiritual selves," the most miraculous parts of ourselves that transcend the physical and mental constructs of our world. In essence, we are working to strengthen our lifelines to the Lord so that we can firmly exist in the essence of God.

There is a concept that I call "alert and caution" to help me identify and deal with mountains that arise in my life or the lives of others. Have you ever confided in someone and told them about a mountain in your life? They probably listened and offered you advice.

Then, the moment they began to tell you about their mountain, they surprised you with the enormity of theirs in comparison to yours! Are you one of those people who slipped and blurted out something like, *"Wow! And I thought I had a problem!"* Well, guess what? The mountains in our lives do not discriminate! They have no regard for any particular category of people. What may be more unsettling to you is that as parents, guardians, or caretakers of others, some of us frequently take on the additional strife of climbing the mountains that exist in the lives of our loved ones while dealing with our own. Regardless of all that is said, done, or read out of the Bible for them, our beloved may still fall by the wayside...with their faith torn to shreds. For them, the question remains, "How do I move my mountain?" Our challenge becomes more difficult as we try to figure out what can we do, as Christians, to help them.

We must bear witness for them and intervene in prayer on their behalves. The Word of Matthew 11:23 is proof that God has given all of His believers the power to move mountains. For this reason, we must guard our faith. The fact that we must remain "alert" in the midst of attacks and negativity can not be emphasized enough! When our faith is fully charged, we are in a position to recognize the "caution" signs for overcoming life's mountains, regardless of their sizes. When we slow down, we can thus observe these caution signs with tender care. We can then proceed with actions that are appropriate for the situations at hand. Only then can we assist our brothers and sisters in name of Christ. We can acknowledge how their mountains have devastated them and driven them down roads leading to their self-destruction. While evil threatens to hold them hostage, please remember that Jesus loves them always! It is not God's desire to have any of His children imprisoned by Satan! So, you must demonstrate a "Christ-like" love for them, serving as outreach resources of ministry and witnesses on behalf of Jesus and the many wonders He has in store for us. Always open your heart and your mind to the Lord's call of duty, for God always works in mysterious ways! Have you ever had a mountain moved from your life while in the midst of helping someone else? I have! What a rush it was for me! Without a doubt, I know that God is awesome!

What follows is a testimony that I would like to share with you. It is one that serves as a very cherished and memorable time of "faith in action" for me.

One day, I met a colleague of mine whom I had not seen for several years. For the sake of his anonymity in this passage, his name will be John. Over the course of our catching up, he told me about several of the "mountains" in his life. He had a great job, but lost it. He had been married, but just undergone a bitter divorce. His children had turned against him. Additionally, the nice home and luxury car that he once owned had come to pass as well. However, his troubles did not stop there. John's father had passed away, a man whom he felt was the only person left for him to confide in. Other family members who could assist him in his time of grief had passed away as well. Thus, as John allowed himself to speak open and honestly with me, I could feel that the sea of life was drowning him. However, there was one new thing in his life that he could be thankful for, a young lady who had come into his life despite the fact that he had begun describing himself as "a broken man who could not see past the trees and darkness of his jungle." After telling me about her, he apologized for taking up my time with his troubles. Yet, I assured him that he was no burden to me. You see, dear reader, I recognized that his words were a "caution" sign for me. The Spirit of Discernment had already "alerted" me that something was worthy of my tender attention prior to our conversing. Regardless of plans I had made for that day, it was my duty to slow down, stop, and then proceed to serve the will of God.

After conversing with John, I prayed to God, and I thanked Him for the opportunity to intervene on his behalf. In the name of the Holy Spirit, I pled that the blood of Jesus would bless John now and forever more. I asked that the vile forces that threatened to break his faith be let loose. Most importantly, I prayed that he would be made whole again, and that his faith would be mended, restored, renewed, and reactivated! I called to the Lord to allow John to take on the whole of the armor of God so that he would walk boldly beyond the dark shadows of his jungle...into an illuminated path set forth for him by none other than the Almighty.

That day, my faith had already allowed me to confirm that John's future was made brighter. When he contacted me a couple of months later saying his life was shaping up for the better, I rejoiced in his testimony. He had gone to several job interviews for which prospects were in place. He was excited to announce to me that he had found the will and the strength rejoin church as well! But the best was yet to come...

Today, John is gainfully employed with a very successful company. His employment opportunity, a blessing from God, has allowed him to buy a new home and a new vehicle. John regained his self-confidence. He asked that young lady who stood beside him in his time of trouble and need to marry him. She is now his God-chosen wife, a wife who kept her faith in the Lord and trust that John would find his way. The illusion of evil manifested by John's mountain had now befallen to the sea of a successful life in the valleys below it. Now John's relationship with his children, although still not perfect, brings promises of an ever-lasting familial bond.

ALL GLORY TO THE LORD, GOD! My friend, my sibling in Christ, remember, we are vessels, the mortal instruments of He who carries us by the faith we have in Him. He helps us to safely land ashore on the thrashing waters made serene by His glory. We are able to run into the welcoming arms of the family of Christ forever more. With the acceptance of Jesus Christ as our Savior, the power of God has given us the miraculous ability to MOVE MOUNTAINS!

Do We Quibble or Get On Track?

You and I are about to embark on a journey as I discuss topics that—for as long as I can remember—have proven to be quite controversial to many people. These topics have also proven to be petty to others. However, in either case, both Christians and non-Christians are involved.

It is a fact that non-Christians are more skeptical when it comes to addressing certain issues or opinions presented by Christians. But—sad to say—much of how non-Christians see things is actually based on encounters with or observations made regarding those who profess to be Christians. I agree that how *we* conduct ourselves is to be considered; however this is not the primary issue at hand. How we conduct ourselves is an exhibition of morals and values that can be showcased by anyone. And I do mean *anyone*!

The Christian is regarded by many as having high standards of expectation of personal conduct, decency, and order. But is it not also true that there are people among non-Christians who display good morals and values as well? Aren't there non-Christians who possess high standards for personal conduct, decency, and order too? The only difference is that there is quibble among shared concepts! That is the primary issue at hand. Through this revelation, I will move on to the true goal of this message. I will define and explain in detail certain topics that I am convinced will benefit everyone, Christian or non-Christian, near or far.

In considering the delivery of my message, I thought of how the comedian might find it necessary to rely on hitting the audience with an opening punch line. I also thought of the minister using a little religious humor to get the congregation to open up to receiving the Word of God. While preliminaries are effective in their own right, I choose to rely on a "head-on" approach for delivering this message. Time and time again, I have observed ongoing quibbles among people when discussing "The Spiritual Gift of Discernment" and "Natural Talents." So, dear reader, shall we try to put this "quibble" to an end? No preliminaries are needed!

As a teacher, I never assessed students on vocabulary tests before making sure I had done my job at teaching the meanings of words. I used them within contextual statements relevant to real-life situations. Just as I have done in the classroon, I clearly define certain words herein that capture distinguishing topics as necessary so that you may truly appreciate this reading.

Let us focus on a general definition of the word **discernment**:

Discernment is the ability, or gift, to hear or read things that are taught, to recognize that a problem exists, and to consider suggestive courses of action.

This ability is extremely beneficial to us. It helps us to determine whether the source behind the things we hear or read is divine, of human nature, or maybe even Satanic. Discernment allows us to perceive what problems exist, even if we cannot easily see what they are on the surface. Then, we develop an acute sense of what actions we should take, even if we do not choose to act accordingly. The Bible supports the fact that "discernment" is one of the spiritual gifts to humans from God in 1 Corinthians 12:10 KJV, as it is described as the "discerning of spirits." Feel free to go back and read the definition and then apply it to its reference in the Bible. There is nothing wrong in making sure that you are grasping the concept. Remember, this is our goal!

Now that we have examined the definition of discernment in the general sense, and we know that it is a gift from God, let us focus on the gifted talents that exist among us.

Natural Talent (Gift)

A "natural talent (gift)" is defined as a genetic outcome or a talent that is acquired through a learning process or some type of training.

by Mrs. Patsy Bazile

Question: "Who can possess this gift?

Answer: Anyone.

Often, we hear people talk about an inherited talent that someone has such as singing, playing an instrument, or being a great orator. People who recognize their own gifts become more effective at using them by taking lessons to improve them. Through faith and the grace of God, we—whether we are Christians or non-Christians—can then "perfect" them. All people who possess unique gifts have similar experiences; but, non-Christians tend to use their gifts for non-Christian purposes. That does not mean, however, that their talents exclude helping others. Let me give you an example. A person with a natural talent of playing music may elect to go to college where they obtain a degree in music. Thereafter, this person may play music for countless audiences and also educate students so that they may achieve their dreams of becoming musical artists as well.

Spiritual Talent (Gift)

A "spiritual talent (gift)" is defined as a talent that is the result of a power that is under the direct dictatorship and authority of none other than the Holy Spirit. Man does not decide on spiritual gifts, nor does man assign spiritual gifts to anyone. You must not, and I repeat, you must not be unclear about this!

Question: "Can anyone receive this gift?

Answer: Well, there is no beating around the bush with this one! No, not anyone, only *believers*.

Romans 12:6 NKJV tells us precisely that spiritual gifts are given by the Holy Spirit, and it is our duty to use them in service to God! As stated in 1 Corinthians 12:4-11 NIV, "there are different kinds of gifts, but the same Spirit distributes them." These gifts are intended to be used at the will of God, "just as He determines."

As I continue to be a vessel for the deliverance of this lesson, I would like to elaborate more on teachings about our human gifts. Thus, in obedience to the Holy Spirit, let me be as clear as possible. Notice that the word *gift* is enclosed in parentheses for the definitions of both "natural talent" and "spiritual talent." This is because of the fact that talent is synonymous with gift in this lesson. Gifts, or talents, come from God whether they are natural or spiritual! So that means that there is a wide open opportunity for *everyone* to "blend" worship, praise, and glorification of Jesus Christ with sharing of our gifts with others. Allow me to explain. Remember the person with the musical natural talent who decided to become a music teacher? Look around, brothers and sisters in Christ, the Minister of Music at your church is a spectacular example!

Discernment is a particular gift of which I am enamored. I rejoice every time I meet a person of faith who is aware that he

by Mrs. Patsy Bazile

or she has the spiritual gift of discernment. Society is filled with temptations and evil influences that attack humanity at every turn in life. Temptations show up everywhere! They are in our homes, in our schools, at our jobs, at our fingertips with technology, and even in the House of God. But for the individual who possesses the gift of discernment, his or her ability serves as an "early warning system" to the body of Christ. The deliverance of this lesson to you, dear reader, urges me to stress to you how the Holy Spirit encourages us to use our spiritual gifts. Somewhere along your spiritual walk you may meet someone, just as I have, who says, "I know I have a spiritual gift, but I just don't get it! I cannot fully understand nor explain it, so...I—I just try to forget about it!" But remember that all willing workers for Christ have the duty of helping people who do not recognize how to tap into the potential of their spiritual gifts. We must not shrug our shoulders at this divine opportunity to encourage and support this person. We should remind this child of God that the gift he or she has is of supernatural origin. Even though forgetting about this gift may seem to be an option, forgetting may not even be possible. It may become apparent to you that many people who recognize that they have spiritual gifts are often so overwhelmed by them that they overlook the fact that their spiritual gifts are governed by the authority of God. He is and will always be in charge! It is your duty to help them to realize that obedience to God is what really matters. In the grand scheme of things, what does it matter that one cannot "fully understand or explain" their spiritual gifts? You are in a leadership role for the teachings of Christ, blessed with the greater perception of knowing how to connect with the Holy Spirit. Share with others that you know and have faith in the fact that God moves without error. Trust that your actions will be guided at His discretion. The impact to our spiritual development is profound when we help those who possess talents, natural or spiritual. In every moment that I live by this testament, I remember the words of my grandmother. She would say, "Cast all of your burdens on the Lord and just allow Him to use you. You will understand it better by and by!"

I am eager to announce to you an "all-point bulletin" in this reading. The writing of my words lends itself to an elaboration on the love Christ has for us. No matter who you are, if you are a believer in Christ, then the Holy Spirit will surround you! At this very moment, some people are saying to themselves, "I have been praying for a long time for God to give me a 'specific' gift, but so far, I haven't received it!" My soul feels that some readers of my words have reached the point where they just want to throw in the towel and give up! But **do not** let the devil win! Beware and never forget that he is aware of what you are feeling. He will trick you and use your weakness as an opportunity to tug at, tarnish, and eventually destroy your faith. But you are a fighter and the bearer of gifts from God! Denounce the devil! Speak boldly right now and say "How dare you, slippery prince of darkness! Get thee behind me, Satan! I bind you right now in the name of Jesus Christ! I rip myself free right now from your bondage and let go of doubts concerning the Lord, my God! My trust is in Him and only Him, on Whom I rely for my breadth of life. I am God's property, and I have no doubt in Him anymore. He is the supplier of all of my needs! No weapon formed against me shall prosper! Amen!" Now…just relax.

Remember the Holy Spirit is in charge, so let Him decide your fate in every action that you take. If you are a believer, and your faith is strong, **you know** that you have a gift. Still in God's divine plan for us, He only makes life clear to us when we are "ready" to see and know what He has in store for us!

All-Point Bulletin from the Word of God

All of us have heard of the word *psychic*. There are some people who claim to be psychics and "revealers" of the future. However, scripture warns us and strongly forbids the exercising of any kind of ill practices regarding our spiritual gifts.

Please read the following justification carefully!

Deuteronomy 18:10-14 NIV says; "Let no one be found among you who sacrifices their son or daughter in the fire, who practices divination or sorcery, interprets omens, engages in witchcraft, or casts spells, or who is a medium or spiritist or who consults the dead. Anyone who does these things is detestable to the Lord; because of these same detestable practices the Lord your God will drive out those nations before you. You must be blameless before the Lord your God."

Dear reader, it is not God's intention for us to waste time "quibbling" over our gifts! We must use them wisely and effectively in our ministries, throughout our testimonies, and on our missions for Him. God will recognize you as a child of His who bears good fruit...the fruit of the righteousness. So what do you say now? Will you quibble, or will you get on track? I'm so glad we agree!

by Mrs. Patsy Bazile

Mr. Intimidation and the Wee Mouse

It's a beautiful day! It's not too hot, not too cold, but somewhere in the middle...just right. In fact, it doesn't feel like any season that I have ever experienced before! The grass is such a beautiful shade of green that it seems unreal. In the air, a sweet aroma caresses the breeze; a scent unlike any other that I have ever detected! Isn't that strange? But that's not all! When I look up at the sky, I am amazed at such beauty! It's an abyss of blue hues and fluffy clouds so white that they are nearly blinding to my sight! Oh, and wait! Can you hear it? There are the sounds of birds singing and dancing about in the trees while a soft melody floats on the air molecules around me. These musical notes tickle my ear drums. Where are those sweet sounds coming from? There are no instruments being stroked near me. And those sounds are so pure in tone that they cannot possibly be created by a mechanical sound system. The melody is so fantastic that I fear I will never tire of listening to it! Never! I can hear the trumpets welcoming me. I'm listening so intently that I now notice how the rhythm is ever so slightly increasing with every stride that I take in this place. And now, another melodic layer is introduced...a flute perhaps. No, a violin, I think. Oh, yes, now I hear it...a harp! But as quickly as I hear those bolstering musical runs, they lower to a faint hum. I have been welcomed to this marvelous place. So now I want to follow the music to the source of its creation! Will I ever find it?

You're not going to believe this: for some reason, I knew that I was coming here! I remember now. Recently, I had an unknown visitor come to me…out of nowhere it seemed. I was not expecting any visitors at all that day. Yet, I received a knock at my door. When I opened it, before I could speak, the stranger smiled at me and said, "I am a messenger for the Lord. Your plea was received, and your actions have been deemed highly favored by Him. Here is your invitation, Redemption, for your heart has revealed your profound transformation. Seek and follow Jesus, for He loves you, and He has not forsaken you! May God be with you." Then, when I rubbed my eyes to make sure I was not dreaming, I opened them to see that my visitor had simply disappeared! A whisper lingered saying, "Do not open the package that I left for you. That is for later. When the time is right, you will know it…"

I looked down at my feet. A box sat there on the floor at my toes. It was the only physical evidence left by the stranger. It was proof that what I had experienced was real. So, I picked up the box, and I put it in my storage closet. Can you believe it? I was not tempted one bit to open my gift. No, I was compelled to be obedient to someone whom I had never before seen or met. Strangely, I knew in that moment I had placed the box exactly where it belonged.

by Mrs. Patsy Bazile

Enough about that; so, here I am! I am in the midst of the most beautiful place I have ever seen! And the magnificence of this place is mind boggling. I am so overwhelmed. I can barely acknowledge the fact that I have not met anyone yet. How odd is this? Should I be worried? If I should be, I can surely tell you I am not! I feel as if I can remain perfectly content right here. So while I settle into my joy, I shall walk a bit more just to see what happens next.

Wait a minute! I see someone coming now. Not to worry, they are still very distant. That gives me more time to ponder the unworldly splendor of this place. There are huge crystal chandeliers with sparkling tinges of glittering lights hanging from beyond the clouds. What is holding them up? There are huge gold columns stretching high into the skies. They go on for miles, maybe to the stars. There are shimmering streets of gold stretching out in various directions. They crisscross in geometric patterns. Like puzzles, they send my mind into a fun-filled frenzy as I try to figure them out. And I do! There is one path that makes its way directly to that enormous mansion sitting on a hill! Oh, how opulent it is! I must get closer. As I set afoot on my journey to that mansion, I notice that the gold surfaces beneath my feet have no scuff marks on them. Amazing! I know that these roads have been well traveled. And still, I am pleased to know that they are perfect roads: no matter which path is taken, they all are graceful, absolutely perfect roads!

I stride onward. Then, I begin to realize just how far away I am from the magnificent abode. Since there is a bench nearby, I decide to take a rest. As I take my seat, I inspect its structure. How brilliant and white it is! It is the most perfect and cleanest bench I have ever seen. Then, when I look up and take note of the nearby road crossing, I notice a sign. "Straightway Boulevard," I say aloud. This is the road that I have been traveling. I must be doing something right!

And remember that other individual who had been very distant from me before? Well, now he is quite a bit closer. It seems that we are the only two occupants in this place; but still, I am not worried! There were so many times in the past when I thought I had something to prove to any and everyone around me. I felt heavier—much heavier—then. I was constantly weighed down by complicated issues, the results of poor decisions I had made and associations with those who only sought to corrupt me. But as I sit here now, I feel so much lighter… light as a feather in fact. I feel as if I could spread a pair of wings on my back, rise up, and take flight! But it's just my imagination…

I exhale. Who needs to imagine anything in a place like this? I focus on the matters at hand, and begin to squint to try to make out who that other individual may be. What? I can't believe it! I think I know who it is? But, it couldn't possibly be him! Such a tiny fellow, I would remember him anywhere. I certainly hope it is him; because if it is, I can finally finish what I set out to do.

§ § §

by Mrs. Patsy Bazile

I have some explaining to do, so allow me to introduce myself to you. My name is Mr. Intimidation. But some have called me by my nickname, Sin. I used to hang out with some buddies of mine and another whom many people—especially Christians—have nothing kind to say about...the devil. I used to think he was pretty cool, being that I met him on the streets of Fool's Paradise, my old stomping ground. But today, I have a new outlook on life. Yet, I remember the first day I met him. Immediately after I met the devil, I became tangled up with him and his unscrupulous ways. I feared him; yet, back then, I clung onto his every word. He offered me things—tempting things—in exchange for my soul! One day, he told me, "I will help you to live up to your name and rule over the lives of others." That was music to my ears, so I gave in. I knew it was wrong. "He wants my soul for all of that?" I asked myself. "Power and control over man," I thought. Back then, I believed it was worth it. So, I followed the devil. He instilled fear in me. He overpowered me as well. And I wanted to do that exact same thing to others.

Life from that point forward changed for me. I controlled the lives of so many people. I made things happen through destruction and manipulation, all at the will of my thoughts and actions. Sure sometimes it became challenging for me to cope with the blood that was shed and the lives that were lost at my resolve. But there was nothing standing in my way. Time and time again, I performed the same acts of devastation. Then they became cyclical, meaningless actions that I had to perform only because of the devil's conniving and sinister plan for me. Soon I began to think to myself, "Was this all that he meant when he said I would 'live up to my name'?" My disappointment was demoralizing.

On one occasion, as I pondered the meaning of my name—Mr. Intimidation—I was interrupted by Wee Mouse, who crossed my path once again. I used to think that Wee Mouse was such a weird little puny creature…so tiny and meek…so weak. But Wee Mouse was also very quick. On that day, he scurried about even quicker when he noticed me standing tall above him. I started to heckle him as I usually did. However, my heart would not allow it that day. I was sad and simply too curious to find out something else. "Wee Mouse," I called, "we need to talk. I need you to help me with something."

Wee Mouse stopped scurrying about, but he kept his distance from me. Then he asked, "Wh-Wh-What do you wa-want, Mr. Intimidation?" He heaved and stood still, trying to slow his thumping heart.

Wee Mouse and I knew each other from past encounters when I tried to bully and destroy him. But Wee Mouse would never allow himself to be defeated by me. He always refused to call me by my nickname…Sin. Avoiding another predictable occasion with him, I figured I would make good use of our time, even though on all other previous accounts, I considered him to be a nerve-wrecking little pest.

"I know that you are very smart, Wee Mouse. So perhaps you can explain the meaning of my name to me," I declared.

Then Wee Mouse responded, "O-Okay, Mr. Intimidation."

He pulled out a pair of tiny reading lenses and then placed them on his face. After pulling out a book from the satchel that hung at his side, he said, "Let's see what the book says. Ok, according to my dictionary, your name means that you behave in manners that cause others to be timid in your presence. Let me be clear: they are afraid of you! And do you know why?"

"Yes, I surely do. But please, do…go on," I urged.

"You are bad and evil," Wee Mouse said. "You corrupt and darken the lives of all whom you come into contact with. For those who are strong in your presence, you beat them down and threaten to weaken them in mind, body, and spirit. For those who are already weak in your presence, you annihilate them. It is all because you want **everything** your way or no way at all! Mr. Intimidation, they are afraid of you, just like I was!"

I closed my eyes, smiled in adoration of myself, and I stuck my chest out. But then I thought to myself, "Wait a minute, what did Wee Mouse just say, 'just like he *was*'?"

I returned to my maniacal sensibilities. I looked at Wee Mouse, and I offered him the meanest facial expression I could give him. Then, I snarled and clawed at him. I was going to rip him apart. But Wee Mouse did not respond the way I thought he should…the way I wanted him to respond. This sent goose pimples down my spine, and it was because no one had responded to me in that manner before.

Wee Mouse just stood there and looked at me. He stared straight into my eyes, and he said, "You know what, Sin? I am glad we met again today! I have waited a long time for this day."

Wee Mouse then took one step toward me. He continued, "Better yet, I am happy that you decided to allow me to enlighten you about the meaning of your name! My dictionary is a great book, but it only reveals what your name implies. It provides profound insight for why people respond to you the way that they do. But it is limited. What I did not tell you is what I learned from Pastor Owl and the powerful book that he teaches from called the Holy Bible."

At this point, Wee Mouse was completely comfortable in my presence. I could not comprehend this!

Wee Mouse went on, "One day, Pastor Owl's wife invited me to their church. She talked to me about how good it is to know God. She shared with me how wonderful it is to belong to the family of His Son, Jesus Christ. And during her husband's sermon, you became the topic of the day! It was right then that I knew God was real. He had come into my heart, and I knew that He would have an answer for how I should respond to you during our next encounter. Now here we are."

"So He is responsible for this? He is responsible for your foolish courage in my presence?" I asked.

"Hush, Mr. Intimidation," Wee Mouse told me. "This time, abide with me. You cannot have your way today. So as I was saying, Pastor Owl opened his Bible, the book of God's Holy Word! He spoke to the congregation about how we should arm ourselves against all evil, and he called our attention to Philippians 1:28 NLT which reads, 'Don't be intimidated by your enemies. This will be a sign for them that they are going to be destroyed, but you are going to be saved, even by God himself!' So you see, whether you be called Intimidation or Sin, I AM NOT AFRAID of you, ANYMORE! I have declared my belief in an Almighty God who says to every believer, 'Come boldly to the throne of grace so that we may obtain mercy and find grace in the time of need' Hebrews 4:16 NKJV. As I have gazed deeply into your fearsome pupils, tarnished by false promises that the prince of darkness has made to you, I declare that 'No weapon that is formed against thee shall prosper; and every tongue that shall rise against thee in judgment, thou shall condemn them, and their righteousness is of the LORD!' Isaiah 54:17 KJV"

I was speechless. But Wee Mouse would not stop.

Next he said, "Sin, as I have renewed strength, and I seek to conform to the ways of the Christian. I humbly take refuge in the presence of the Lord! In my obedience to Him, I remember his word which tells me, 'Never take my own revenge, for I am God's beloved, in order that I leave room for the wrath of my Lord' Romans 12:19 (KJV). So, it is with that love of God that I shall pray for you. See, this is what children of God do. I shall pray for you because I am bound by compassion for your soul, a soul that summons total destruction, lest you be set free of the bondage that has imprisoned you by your own nickname, 'Sin!'"

I was completely overwhelmed, and I fell into a stupor. Barely conscious, I heard a voice say to me, "Someone has been praying for you. Despite the wickedness of your ways, someone has allowed himself to peer into your heart. He has interceded for you, and the Lord has found favor in him and his noble will. However, Intimidation, you must make changes in your life so that God can find favor in you as well. These are your instructions!"

When I regained my full consciousness, I felt weightless and as though I could ride a wistful breeze into the clouds. I no longer felt as if I were some wild predator on the prowl! I felt humble! Somehow I had made it back to my home, only to find myself standing in front of a mirror. I looked upon it, and examined my reflection. I no longer saw a frown and ferocious expression eager to push others away from me in fear. I saw sorrow. I was indeed sorry for all that I had done to harm others, and I knew then that I needed help from someone greater than myself. I needed the help of the Lord for redemption! Tears began to fall from my eyes. Then I cried unto the Lord saying, "Lord, please save me! I have surrendered all to your will!"

Days after that, I tried to get in touch with my buddies to tell them about my newly found faith. I wanted them to know how I had come to acknowledge the grace of God and His blessed assurance. However, for some reason, I repelled them as soon as I came into contact with them! I attempted to get close to them to speak of my good news, but all they could do is shriek away from me and cover their eyes. An unknown force prevented me from going near them and kept them from coming near me! They could not even bear the sight of me! *Things had changed.*

"What is wrong with you guys?" I asked. "I have so much to tell you."

They were so eager to disregard anything I had to say to them. The only words that one of my buddies had for me is, "Get away! The devil is mad at you! You better watch out, Sin. You better watch your back."

I was no longer concerned about the devil. In fact, when that name "Sin" was spoken, I wanted to turn around to see if anyone else was standing behind me. I no longer honored that nickname. I only became concerned with seeking forgiveness from those I had hurt so much—those I had hurt for so very long.

§ § §

Today, I can honestly say that I have spent a long time asking for forgiveness. I have done the work to appeal to those whom I have hurt in my dreadful past. Thankfully, I have succeeded at contacting nearly everyone on my list. Yet the most important one remains to be found, Wee Mouse. Now I wonder if I'm too late. I think I know where he is, but the question is: *will* I ever get there too?

I tried to find Wee Mouse. He used to live on the far end of the city in a "refined" area, as some might say. Determined to seek his pardon of my most ungodly past ways, I traveled to Salvation Oaks. I knocked on his door; but no one answered. I peeped through a front window. The place was still and serene. The kindness of his heart still lingered in the tranquility of the grand domicile. Yet, the place looked empty. It only seemed to stand there now in memoriam of Wee Mouse's previous existence there. So, with my head hung low, I started walking away from his abandoned abode. Then I noticed something on the ground. It was misplaced among the roots of some shrubbery. Someone must have dropped it there. When I picked up the postcard, I noticed that it had the most fantastic scenery on it. How was that image ever taken by a camera? It was almost holographic in nature. In gold letters stretched across the top of it were the words, "City of God."

That's where Wee Mouse is! I knew it. Wee Mouse is in the blessed Kingdom of the Lord! Oh, how would I ever get there?

It's okay. I am blessed now. Here I am, sitting on this beautiful snow white bench on the corner of Straightway Boulevard and Faithful Drive. It's okay! I am favored! I am in this fabulous place where all of the streets are paved with gold. Come to think of it, I am right in the middle of that scene I saw! I'm in the postcard, that postcard that Wee Mouse lost!

That sign up ahead, look at what it says! "City of God," I have made it! That mansion on the hill I see…the House of the Lord awaits me! And then I see him…Wee Mouse! He is the stranger who has made his way to me. Just when I thought I would never see him again, faith has prevailed! And now I cannot keep my composure. A stream of tears rolls down my face. I nearly fall to my knees, but when Wee Mouse approaches me, I feel the love of Christ in his heart. The Spirit of God gives me strength to speak.

I say to Wee Mouse, "Forgive me. I never thought I would ever see you again. Please accept my humble apology for all harm I have attempted against you. Wee Mouse, I beg for your forgiveness!"

"I forgave you long ago," he says. "And Jesus has too. He told me He was eager to dwell in your heart. Your invitation to accept his grace has brought you to this magnificent place…the land of the Almighty…the Omnipotent Creator."

Then I hear the faint clattering of something beside me.

"The box, it's there for you. You are ready," Wee Mouse says. "You shall be attired in your heavenly garments, and the Holy Spirit shall give you wings! Welcome to the City of God. Let's go to our Father's kingdom. And from now on, your name shall be 'Redemption'."

by Mrs. Patsy Bazile

Do You Ever Wonder WHY?

Lately, I have been meeting a lot of people who are still pondering the big "WHY?" in either one or several aspects of their lives. Usually, the major challenges that arise in their lives are what cause them to focus on it. Many of these people are Christians—people of faith—who are very active in their churches. Most of them are working people, with families, nice homes, and nice vehicles. Some have great jobs, while others are retired or operate small businesses with the hopes that they will have a financial cushion to rely on during their retirement years. So, all in all, aside from living "normal" lives, whatever those are considered to be, these folks always end up asking themselves, "Why?" No one is free from burdens to bear.

I began noticing several years ago that after I met some people, some for the very first time, I would have small talk with them—conversations that involved the divulgence of small details about themselves, which would then inflate into more profound and personal exchanges. At that point, the contemplation of "WHY?" would then spread to me. Why was I chosen to be *the one* for them confide in? They did not know me. As uncomfortable as I would sometimes become, I still listened to them. I was compelled to do so. Let me assure you that there was no intent of personal gain on my behalf. I was not listening for the mere purpose of entertainment or material for gossip with others. I knew that something was manifesting inside of me. I could not really explain what was happening. All I know is that despite whatever discomfort I may have felt during the beginning of those conversations, it would soon pass as my mind and soul would give way to calmly receiving them. My own responses would amaze me. I would find myself offering words to them that were automatically comforting, encouraging, and uplifting. My words did not always seem to be those that they wanted to hear; however, my words were most often well received and very appreciated.

I was born in a home where Jesus was no "secret." My Mother—bless her sweet soul—always taught us that it was important to believe in the Lord, go to church, and treat others, especially our elders, with love, politeness, and utmost respect. We would even have church at home during the week! Bible study was required in our home. Mom would gather everyone in the kitchen, and we would sit at the table, never for obnoxiously long periods of time, but long enough to accomplish the primary goal of centering our family within the omnipotence of the Lord. One of my brothers would be asked to find a scripture to read for kicking off our Bible study roundtable. Then another brother of mine would be told to lead us in singing an opening song. We would sing hymns and make joyful noise in our house of God! We would even have an altar prayer. Mom would explain how important it was for us to confess our sins to God. She told us that we needed to ask for His forgiveness and His help to refrain from sinning in the future. Before ending Bible study, someone would offer the closing prayer, and then we would sing "Till We Meet Again." As the youngest child and baby girl, I often was not given a lot of responsibility throughout our Bible study proceedings. But when it came to listening to the Word of God and responding to questions, I was never exempted from those activities. Mom made sure of it with the many times she caught me off guard with her verbal quizzes! Whenever I was fidgety and a bit too busy at the table, she would give me that "look," the one that expressed to me with no words, "Listen." At a very young age, I was being trained to LISTEN FOR COMPREHENSION TO PROVIDE A SUBSEQUENT RESPONSE!" At that age, I did not realize that my mother was instilling in me the true intent of listening, which excluded gossip and misuse of information for reckless entertainment.

As I got older, I became more aware of the fact that while I enjoyed talking with and listening to people, there was always a kind of intuitive alert within my spirit that I could not ignore. I felt as if I could discern the trivial words of some people from the meaningful ones of others who needed to confide in me. This feeling inside of me really did not bother me; however, there were many times I wondered, "WHY? Why me?"

Over the years, I found myself reflecting on words that my mother spoke to me: "No matter how much people instill within us regarding God and the importance of believing in Him, people must accept Jesus for themselves."

Quite some time ago, I joined a church where my husband had been a member. The obvious reason for my joining would, of course, seem to be my husband's membership, but this was not the primary reason. As I sat in the congregation one day, I *listened* to the pastor offer a testimony. I observed his clear and candid honesty as he spoke to us—his children, he would say—about his past life and previous bad deeds. The pastor told us that when God shows up in our lives, He does this so that we may witness his glory and possess a personal testimony of truth. We can unite on His behalf with other "testifiers," and we can then bring others into the Family of Christ! He was an honest man: I had never before heard a minister be so blunt about not always being a Christian, but instead a rebellious soul who pushed others away even though they may have only had his best interest at heart. He explained that his Christianity began when he met an older preacher who saw him unlike anyone else could. Tears came to my eyes when the pastor said that the older preacher pointed out his flaw of "fighting a burning compassion and love for others." Our pastor had been allowing the devil to blind him. In his early life, he could not accept his "true calling." But as the older preacher mentored him, our pastor allowed God to enter his heart. Then God commanded, "Run no more!" Reflecting on his past, our Pastor testified in his sermon, "Don't tell me what the Lord can't do!" The church lit up with praises and shouts of "Amen!" On that day, I knew that I had to join the church. It was then that I could fully acknowledge the love and acceptance of Jesus for myself. And as far as the question of "why me?" was concerned, an answer began to formulate for me, although other questions of "WHY?" would soon follow.

by Mrs. Patsy Bazile

My first marriage was devastating. It was worse than I let everyone else around me know. During that marriage, I can remember asking myself, "WHY?" I could not understand what I was doing wrong. Why was I being subjected to the things I was going through? I would ask myself over and over, "Should I stop talking so much?" "Should I ignore the hurtful things that were being said about me and my family?" "Is there more that I should be doing to save my marriage?" "If so, what are those things?" Then, I would hear answers to these questions in the back of my mind: "Talk and speak what is on your mind; no one is perfect. Some things are just too hurtful to ignore; that is not your problem. There is nothing more you can do because you are already giving it your best shot." Nevertheless, the longer my marriage continued was the worse things got. Then one day, I realized it was over. That very night, I prayed, and as clear as a bell, a deep voice spoke to me saying, "It was over quite some time ago, but you are trying to prove to others that it could work. Now walk in my will and my way." I shared this occurrence with my Pastor. He told me, "I know you've been through a lot, but God has something better ahead for you. The voice that you heard was the voice of God. He speaks to us when we need Him most. Be patient, and things will work out. In all that you do, do so for the Lord." I will never forget this. Yes, it was true that I was trying to prove to others that my marriage would work. And silly me, I did not realize that many people could already see that it was doomed.

So "WHY?" Why did I have to go through this?

After my divorce, I continued working as a paraprofessional within the elementary education system. But I also began pursuing a bachelor's degree in elementary education. A coworker of mine was very instrumental in persuading me to do so. He had been teaching for a while, and he had been very good at it. I always enjoyed my opportunities to observe him as he taught. I liked the way his kids remained disciplined when I watched his class. Over time, we became friends. Then, he began sharing some things about himself to me. I "listened" to him, and I also shared some of my experiences with him. We learned that we had a lot in common. In many ways, we had faced many of the same challenges. I tried to encourage him, telling him that he might be able to overcome the challenges that he was experiencing in life. I never allowed myself to be driven by self-gain or to use any of our confidential conversations to do harm to anyone involved.

As I think back on the beginning of my relationship with my coworker, I know that our other co-workers and friends may have figured out that we were becoming more than just friends. Personally, I never focused on it because there were still too many questions of "WHY?" More importantly, I was excited about the potential that he noticed in me as he encouraged me to go back to school and pursue a bachelor's degree. As time went on, trust and love grew between us. Then one day, he laid it all out on the table and told me exactly how he felt about me. I felt as if our friendship was meant to be: this man was put in my life for a reason!

by Mrs. Patsy Bazile

The day I graduated from Southern University, he was there for me. He was proud of me. My mom could not be in attendance because she had been ill, yet I knew that she was in her home cheering me on. My son was not in attendance because I did not want him to miss school. He was nearing his college graduation date as well. But when I looked out into the crowd and saw the smile of my friend's face, I saw the smiles of all the people I loved the most.

Approximately one year after my graduation, I married my friend, my present husband. The day I remarried was an unforgettably beautiful day! I felt beautiful too. Most of all, I felt so very blessed. Just before our wedding, I remember feeling nervous as well. When my son asked if I were, I pretended as if I were not. But there was no denying it. I still chuckle inside to this day when I think of my son and my jittery laughter right after a plate fell out of my hand as a result of his question.

My husband and I are still together. We do not have the perfect marriage, but no one does. What I can say for sure is that we have a marriage that was united by God. But still, the question of "WHY?" exists. WHY did I have to go through the tribulations of my previous marriage? WHY did my husband have to go through the previous perils of his? And WHY did we have to overcome the latent remnants of our previous experiences which crept into our current marriage?

Because I am older and wiser, I can reflect on my upbringing, one that urges me to believe in God and trust in His wondrous glory.

I can think of the words that our pastor said when we consulted him: "The God we serve has given us ALL free will. We are free to ask for His help while making important decisions in our lives. But we are also free to make decisions on our own. This does not mean that He will choose to not bless us with every blessing He has in store for us. When we make choices and decisions on our own, this slows the timing of our receiving them. But when He gives them to us, there is blessed assurance that we know we are receiving our blessings from Him at the right time. There is acknowledgement that we have learned from the error of our ways, and we know what it is to be truly grateful. In comparison, we can recognize what God has done for us as opposed to those things we have tried to do all on our own." He continued, "Trust me, I know that it is true in His Word that 'the Lord looks beyond our faults and sees our needs' and in yours and your husband's case, God has allowed you to make mistakes. By the time you two got together, you both had experienced storms in your lives, faced many challenges and let-downs, deceptions, accusations, persecutions, feelings of loss and despair, and other adversities. God used all of these mishaps to strengthen your faith in Him. Despite *any* evil forces or influences that would find their way into your current marriage, none would prevail for 'What God puts together, no man puts asunder (Mark 10:9 KJV)'."

I thank the Lord for all of my blessings on a daily basis. Even if my lips do not utter the words, I know that Jesus understands what is in my heart. I thank God for all of the storms I have encountered in life, because I can appreciate the sunshine that much more! I thank Him for the many hurtful words that have been said to me in the past because I now have the strength to endure any other storms that are yet to come. I also I thank God for the friends who have forsaken me, because now I am able to discern among people who now come into my life for ill will or true friendship.

I have no doubts about God's blessings. I thank Him for the people who have had my best interest at heart and those people who have not. There were lessons to be learned from my encounters with both. With every lesson that I have learned, wisdom has accompanied it. Rest assured that wisdom is an amazing and wonderful gift from God! He has a reason for *everything* He does, for HE MAKES NO MISTAKES! Whatever He allows us to go through occurs for a reason. This is what I share with individuals who are facing challenges and crises in their lives. Just hold on and keep the faith because the race is often not won by the swiftest…many times the winner is the one who endures to the end (Matthew 24:13 NKJV).

Yes, we *all* wonder "WHY?" from time to time. But the more you learn about Jesus and stride in your Christian walk, the stronger your relationship will be with Him. You will listen as He speaks to your mind and your heart. You will humble yourself and allow yourself to feel His presence. You will empty your spiritual vessel, and He will fill you up again! You will always wonder "WHY," my friend. It is because there is always something wonderful and new to learn about God, the Almighty and Eternal Creator, each day! Learning never stops, but your questions of "WHY?" will *finally* receive their answers!

Zera, Daughter of Faith

Author's Message to the Reader

Dear Reader,

This book would not be complete without a story that truly conveys my commitment to my faith. As I am quite sure you already know, life has a way of presenting challenges to us that shake our faith during random moments in our lives. Those challenges come in many forms, and they may last any length of time ranging from minutes to a full lifetime! As for most of us, the longer the challenge lasts makes for the more vulnerable we become. We may begin to wane physically, mentally, and spiritually due to all of the pressure and strife that we endure.

I hope that I have made it quite clear in this book that Satan is analyzing every move and stammer that we make. He is devising a plan to attack us and use every one of our weaknesses against us. And when it comes to our faith, he tries as hard as he can to defeat us.

Over the passing years, I have spoken to many people who shared with me the fact that they have either dealt with or are still dealing with long-term challenges in their lives. These challenges have involved friends, family, work life, and, in some cases, their overall livelihood. Yet, many of these people have been what I would identify as strong people! So I caution you, reader, that even the most resilient people among God's children can become overwhelmed and overtaken by the storms of life.

They, too, may develop feelings of hopelessness leading to despair and pressure… and eventually complete capitulation. "Whatever will be…will be," they might say, without fully realizing that they have alerted Satan with a bright, yellow caution light! "Come to me, Satan," they beckon with their pulsating yellow light, which is on the verge of turning green! Then that is when the devil takes aim and locks his target on their souls. But have no fear, I urge you. You must never forget that you too have a powerful weapon in your arsenal. Counter attack! The Holy Bible is there for you whenever you need it. It shall strengthen your muscles, stretch your faith, and nourish your soul with the mana you need to persevere.

> *"But those who wait on the Lord*
> *Shall renew their strength;*
> *They shall mount up with wings like eagles,*
> *They shall run and not be weary,*
> *They shall walk and not faint."*
> *Isaiah 40:31 NKJV*

Remember the Bible verse above as you read on. What comes next is the last story that I have to share with you in this book, "Metaphors of Faith, Words of a Praying Woman."

§ § §

My Dearest Friend, Zera Faith

Zera Faith is her name. She is a Christian woman, five years my junior—just young enough for me to sometimes feel comfortable mentoring her as our friendship blossomed over the years. Every now and again, I would help her in times of need when my few additional years spent on this Earth yielded pearls of wisdom for me to share. However, as with any mentor-mentee relationship, our roles would sometimes reverse, and the mentee would teach me something that my temporal wisdom failed to reveal. I have always been extremely appreciative of those moments. They have afforded me the opportunity to see life through a different set of lenses. And I have always cherished my friendship with Zera because—befitting to her last name—she possesses bountiful faith in the Lord. She is generous and very caring at heart. She remains ever modest and humble. She is indeed one of my dearest friends, if not the dearest. So I must not let this go unsaid: what a phenomenal sister of mine in Christ she is!

A long time ago, Zera once told me the meaning of her first name. In Hebrew, "Zera" means "seed." And as I reveal the details of this story to you, you will learn just how beautifully appropriate it is. Zera is a blessing, a gardener who plants seeds of hope in everyone around her. So, dear reader, allow this story to plant roots of hope within you too. May you be profoundly and infinitely inspired!

§ § §

The Faithful Dream

Some years ago, Zera called me up one morning. She asked if I could meet her for lunch that day. In her voice, I could hear modulations of urgency. Accordingly, I obliged to fulfill her request. I proposed an early supper right after work, instead of a rushed and abbreviated lunch date. That would give us more time to catch up and unwind. I just knew in my spirit that our discussion was going to take a while.

That evening, I arrived at the restaurant first. Zera arrived ten minutes later due to heavy traffic. We shared small talk, joked, and caught up on our recent happenings. Then we moved on to spiritual topics—soul stirring gab!

"Are you still writing that book that you told me about?" she asked.

"Yes, I am, and I'm so thankful that the Lord has urged me to do this."

"I bet you are!" she continued. "You're so dedicated to helping people find their way to Jesus."

"That's right, Zera, I am," I agreed. My heart grew warmer as I spoke those words. "Nothing makes me happier. I think it's a calling for me."

"Well, that's why I have something to share with you," she responded. "I—I just need to know that you are open to it."

She was quite reserved, but I wanted to encourage her to continue; therefore, I said, "Of course I'm open! And I know this is going to be good."

Zera beamed with happiness, and she immediately spilled. "Well, it all came to me in a dream," she said. "And I think this is going to be good for your book."

She continued by telling me that she was certain about her faith in God; yet, she had begun to doubt her strength. Zera prayed to God asking Him to keep her faith strong. Still, she continued to wonder if she could remain focused…forever unyielding. Should hardships arise in her life, would she know how to handle and conquer them? Would she remain vigilant in the light of Christ? Should misfortunes arise with her family, would she let her earthly bonds to them overshadow her faith in God?

"I really love the Lord," Zera said. "They say He will never put more on us than we can bear. But sometimes life becomes so overwhelming. And the challenges that come can crush even the strongest of us all. See, I just wanted God to give me a sign regarding my faith. I wanted to know how resilient I am in His name…not only for my sake, but also for that of my family and friends as well."

Between her words, I searched my purse, and I found a pen and a notepad. It was time for me to take notes.

by Mrs. Patsy Bazile

"So God answered my prayer in this dream I'm about to tell you about," Zera affirmed. "And this is how it went…"

Zera was whirled back in time, to the rural countryside of her youth. She was standing in the kitchen of the small shotgun house where she grew up. She marveled at her nostalgic surroundings. They were just as she remembered them, pot belly stove and all. Something was baking, and it smelled delicious. The aroma of her mother's tea cakes tickled her nose with dazzling sensations. But she did not tarry there. Zera walked out of the kitchen and into the family room. The wood-burning fireplace accommodated a small flickering flame. Zera felt no heat dissipating from it, but she noted how beautifully the embers danced about within it. Through the family room she walked toward the four small bedrooms that were lined up ahead. Just as she remembered, she got a clear view through every room straight to the back door. And then poof! Instantaneously, Zera found herself standing in the front yard, looking up at the clear blue sky, basking in the radiance of the sunlight. It did not retain her attention. She looked over at the front porch of her tiny home.

"The swing," she said, interrupting her recollections. "The swing on that porch was so special to me when I was a girl. Momma and Daddy would sit there with their coffee or wine, swinging away… swinging their troubles away."

"How sweet, Zera," I said. "That's beautiful."

"Anyone from a mile away could see just how much they loved each other. That porch was their sacred space. Even I saw how much they enjoyed each other's company. I felt safe as they guarded our home…right there, swinging on that front porch," Zera said. She then continued to tell me about the dream.

> *Out of thin air, younger versions of her parents, Mr. and Mrs. Faith, materialized on the swing. They sat there just like they had so long ago, with love-soaked sparkles in their eyes. Zera stared at them, and at that moment, she realized that they could not see her. They just continued to sit, rocking, and gazing into the depth of each other's soul. They talked about nothing serious, yet still important just the same. Zera's heart and mind could never forget just how much she loved seeing her parents together. They were profoundly yoked and meant to be. Zera could see this, even in her dream.*

> *Suddenly, Zera was transformed into a younger version of herself as well. She was a four-year-old child. And she was no longer standing in the front lawn of the shotgun house. Instead, she stood in the family room with her parents. She looked up at them. They looked back down at their first born. Then, her mother said to her in a soothing voice, "You have always been a content child, even as a baby. Your compassion and blessings will surely spread."*

by Mrs. Patsy Bazile

Zera's father hurled her up into the air! "That's Daddy's little girl!" he happily shouted with pride and joy. "She's going to make us so proud!"

"What a curious one our baby girl is, always gazing at people and such," Mrs. Faith then said. She caressed Zera's childish face and continued, "She doesn't seem to be impressed by them at all, but she is…"

Mrs. Faith's voice ceased, but Zera continued by saying, "I am seeing things within them that no one else can see."

"You know what?" Zera asked me.

"What?" I returned.

"Throughout my entire life, I have always felt as if I had a deep connection with people upon first meeting them. It's like I can feel their energy and their emotions," Zera revealed.

"I can see that. I know that you have a gift," I confirmed. "When I talk to you sometimes, Zera, I can tell that you understand exactly what I say or what I mean even when you don't have first-hand experience with what I'm telling you."

"Really? Well, I believe my gift was confirmed in that dream."

"I don't doubt it. The Lord was speaking to you," I stated.

After Mr. and Mrs. Faith spoke to Zera in the living room in her dream, she found herself peering downward into a crib. A baby was lying there within it.

"Hi, Max," Zera said. He was the Faiths' second-born child, Maximus Faith.

He just smiled and giggled at Zera's greeting. Then looking downward at Max with love, Mrs. Faith began to speak.

"That boy has always been a lively one, so energetic… always going at everything in life with full force. He practically kicked his way out of the womb and into the world!" She chuckled with hope and assurance. "Zera, I know that he will always be challenged by the ways of the world. But you will take care of him, won't you, baby?"

At the end of Mrs. Faith's request, Zera nodded in obedience. Then, her parents faded away into darkness while the flame in the fireplace grew and whipped. It offered some light to see.

Then, a strange thing happened! A ball of fire bounced off the burning logs and onto the living room floor! That fire then bounced into the crib with Max and moved all about him.

Its final resting place was Max's forehead. There it subsided, but it illuminated his tiny body like a light bulb! Uncomfortable with this odd occurrence, Max offered a somber grimace. He stood up and leaned against the railing of his crib. Then he pointed out into the distance. Zera turned to see what had caught his attention. That is when the living room wall across from them came tumbling down. Scenes that spanned Max's life appeared for them to see, and those scenes played like the frames of cinematic drama. Zera saw how troubled Max had been in his adolescent years. She saw how he broke rules and disobeyed their parents' wishes. Zera came to realize that Max was easily frustrated all too often in life. And she took note at how he had no patience for learning life lessons; yet, Max wanted the world to change per his every desire.

I know why I saw Max surrounded by fire in my dream," Zera said.

"Why? What did all that fire illuminating his body mean?" I asked.

"Well, Mom was very deliberate with the names she gave us. Just like she said in my dream, Max is always going at things in life with full force, not really taking into consideration the repercussions for his actions."

"Okay, I see."

"Yes," she said. "Max is a just a natural born attention-getter. He's always eager for life to surrender to his whims and fancies. The fire brightened him up only to cause him pain and discomfort."

"Wow. Okay, that makes sense," I said. I was amazed at how much connotation was clearly evident in Zera's dream.

"Yes. You see the fire in my dream unfortunately reminded me just how much of a burning desire Max has to make his way through life on his own terms…often to his own detriment."

Zera then took in a deep breath and said, "That brother of mine has so much potential; but he stands in his own way sometimes. Ever since he was a child, everything had to be done to his taste or particular liking. He's so smart, and in school making straight A's was nothing for him to accomplish. He would just give up if he didn't like a class or the teacher who taught it. And now, he sees that life after law school is very different." Zera paused. "He can't seem to pass the bar exam, and he is so disappointed with the turn his life has taken."

"That's terrible, Zera," I said. "I pray that he overcomes those challenges the devil has thrown in his way."

"I do too," Zera said, and then she went on to say more about her dream.

by Mrs. Patsy Bazile

When Zera decided to look back over at Max in his crib, she noticed that he was no longer there. In fact, the crib and the entire family room had disappeared. In their place was a brightly lit hospital room. Mrs. Faith lay in a hospital bed holding a newborn baby girl, Aeria, the youngest and last born sibling of Zera. As Mrs. Faith lay there holding her baby girl, she smiled and kissed the infant on her forehead. But Aeria cried and fidgeted wildly in her mother's arms.

"Shhhhh, sweet girl," Mrs. Faith said. "Everything will be okay."

Aeria wailed even more, and Mrs. Faith could not calm her down. She continued to bounce about in her mother's arms while a gentle breeze blew open one of the hospital room windows. The sheer white curtains suddenly sailed about the room, and then the length of them stretched all the way to Mrs. Faith's hospital bed. Those curtains snatched Aeria right out of her mother's arms, but Mrs. Faith did not panic. She simply allowed the curtains to swathe her newborn baby and take her out of the window! When the white curtains released Aeria, she did not fall. She floated and laughed, and she glided among the gentle breezes up to the fluffy clouds of freedom above!

"Dear girl," Mrs. Faith said to Zera. "Your sister has always had a mind of her own…so carefree…and lost. But you,

Zera, keep her in your heart and prayers always. Don't worry. You will never fail her."

As Mrs. Faith reached over to Zera to caress her face, everything around Zera began to vanish. Zera looked down at her feet, and noticed that she was then standing on a freshly cut lawn kissed with the mist of morning dew. She felt as if she was still in a younger body, but this time she was a little older, approximately eleven years old. The lawn on which she was standing was that of her childhood grade school. The building looked exactly the same: it was a small, pale green wooden building, very modest in size, but extremely important to the surrounding community. Zera walked to the main entrance of the school. She walked past the tiny principal's office and front desk immediately to her left. She looked at the unisex bathroom to her right as she continued strolling forward. Then she moved beyond the kitchen area, and past the recreation room in which she had so much fun during her grade school years, either participating in physical exercise classes or school plays. Finally, Zera walked into the school classroom. It was the largest room in the small schoolhouse. It was also the only classroom within the school because it served as the learning center for every grade level. The classroom was dark and dank. But Zera was not alone within it for long. Instantly, students began to pop up all around her. Some of their faces were familiar. However, most of them were not. Some of them were even blurry or distorted. And while the students appeared around Zera and encircled her, her two siblings appeared beside her as well.

by Mrs. Patsy Bazile

"Nan, nanny, boo, boo! Nan, nanny, boo, boo!" the students chanted.

"Look at their clothes," said one of the kids. *"They wore that yesterday! They wore that yesterday!"*

"It's like I was reliving those torturous grade school years again," Zera declared. Her eyes began to water a bit. "The principal and teachers kept all of us in line for the most part. But they couldn't watch every single thing that happened throughout the school. Sometimes those children were mean and disrespectful to my brother, my little sister, and me…because we sometimes wore second-hand clothes or hand-me-downs."

"That's aweful," I said. "I'm sure that was very painful for you."

Zera nodded in agreement. Then she continued with the description of her dream.

Zera looked down at Max. He appeared to be approximately seven years old. He was frowning and yelling words that she could not interpret in her dream. He was also frantically swinging his arms. When he attempted to run into the crowd and attack the spiteful students, Zera pulled him backward by the tail of his shirt. She then looked down at Aeria who was crying profusely as she held tightly to the leg of her older sister. Zera

105

kept her siblings within her grasp. She did not attempt to reflect the students' poor actions, for she knew that she was abiding by the teachings of her parents, just as she was taught to do. In her dream, even though the students began to call Zera "scary cat" just as they had done so long ago in reality, she did not fret.

Through the crowd emerged an adult wearing a bright white suit. Initially, as this man made his way through the students, Zera thought that he was Mr. Phillips, the grade school principal. However, as he got closer to her, the bright white light from his suit blinded her. That light was so bright that it began to conceal the face of the man. He stopped and stood in front of Zera and her siblings. His light formed a dome over them. Then he gently raised his right hand and waved it in front of the mischievous students. They begin to disappear. One by one, they vanished, and then Zera's heart filled with joy.

Oh, wow, Zera," I said. "That was the Lord! You are blessed. He has shown you favor in your dream!"

"I think so," Zera responded. "And I can't even describe how I felt. It's like I knew that I was dreaming, but I could feel His presence all around me!"

"That's amazing!" I said with excitement. "Go on! Please continue."

by Mrs. Patsy Bazile

Suddenly, Zera found herself, along with her entire family, sitting in the congregation of a church. She heard music playing, hands clapping, and choir members singing. There was no roof on the church. Sunrays beamed in from above. Zera could not comprehend the words of the song, but she felt vibrant and excited because the melody was the best she had ever heard. Then, Zera saw her father sitting with the rest of the deacons on the front pew of the church. He was waving his hands about, inspiring the other deacons around him to listen to his words of mentorship, compassion, and counsel. Then she saw her mother on the deaconess pew. She and the other ladies were glowing with pride, holding their hands in the air to praise the Almighty! Zera and her siblings sat together only two rows behind their parents, and they rejoiced in all of the worship around them.

"The church had always been at the root of our family," Zera said. "In my dream, I was reminded of this glorious blessing. Church was the very foundation that made my home one of morals and values, the same ones that I so deeply cherish to this day."

The church instantly froze in time. Zera rose from her seat. The expressions of joy acquired by splendid church service became affixed on the faces of everyone except her. When she looked at her father's face, he seemed to possess an expression of joy slightly diminished by a look of urgency and discomfort. He looked as if something was ailing him.

Zera told me, "I remember that look. It was that very same look that he would sometimes get on his face that revealed how tired he was. Daddy was weary at times. I could see it. But he was extremely determined to provide for us and make the life for us that he dreamed of. He worked so hard back then!"

Zera glared into Mr. Faith's face; he was still motionless. She then saw lines and wrinkles cut deep into his face, neck, and hands. Additionally, soot began to darken his complexion.

"It was the same soot from the warehouse that Daddy used to work at," Zera said to me.

"Interesting," I replied back to her.

Out of the deep wrinkles that formed on Mr. Faith's body in Zera's dream, green vines began to sprout. He was able to move at that point.

"I will not be an infidel in the eyes of the Lord!" he said to Zera in the dream. *"I do as I must and as I should…to take care of my family…to take care of you, my sweet daughter."*

"You know, all I could think of when my father told me this in my dream was 1 Timothy 5, verse 8," Zera said to me. "But if any provide not for his own, and specially for those of his own house, he hath denied the faith, and is worse than an infidel," she recited. "Daddy has always been so dedicated to us."

I then said her, "You're father is good man, a man of God, Zera."

"He sure is," she agreed. And then she continued telling me about her dream.

Everything around them was still motionless. But from behind her father— who was now transformed into a hardy tree firmly planted in front of her, with strong branches overreaching her in protection—Mrs. Faith emerged.

"Don't worry about your father," she said. "I'll take care of him, and God will too. So you go on, baby. You have got to go farther."

The ground beneath Zera disappeared, then she freefell through an abyss. As she fell, she saw images from her life. She saw herself graduating from high school. She then saw herself working at a local drug store to put herself through college. Zera saw the honors that she had received throughout her educational years. She even saw her college degree flash before her very eyes. Then she saw the Bible. She saw the pages within it with scriptures written across them. Then one scripture stood out most:

'Let us hold fast the professions of our faith without wavering, for He is faithful that promised (Hebrews 10:23 KJV).'

"I read that verse nearly every day," Zera said to me. "I also read Isaiah 2:11 (NIV) that says, 'The lofty looks of man shall be humbled, and the haughtiness of men shall be bowed down, and the Lord alone shall be exalted in that day.' I know that I must remain faithful so that I may be blessed. And the Bible also tells me that when I am blessed, I shall not be arrogant, so that even more blessings can come."

"Amen, Zera!" I said. "You are preaching now!

We both had a chuckle.

"I have asked the Lord to place me in his grace and favor. I know that I must be my best so that I can offer my best to others."

"Yes, you can try. And you're right. God has in His power to make you the very best you can be," I said.

"Yes, God is good. And my faith is strong. I know that through Him, I am made stronger. I am determined to not only help myself, but also my parents and my siblings."

"Good things are coming for you, Zera. Because you are looking out for others as well as yourself, I know that God will definitely bless you beyond your imagination as time progresses. You just wait! I know He will," I declared. Then I anxiously said, "So, tell me what happened next in your dream. You were falling, and then what happened next?"

"Well, that's when my dream completely changed pace…"

Years had flown by. Zera's dream was no longer about the past; it focused on moving toward her future. She observed scenes from her life depicting her metrication through her nursing school curriculum. She saw herself receiving her Master's degree in nursing, and her subsequent advancement in her career as a chief nursing officer with a reputable health care facility in the city where she currently lived.

But as she looked out and beyond the horizons of the city, she saw lights beckoning to her. On one side of her, she could see patients calling her name, saying, "Please don't go, please don't go. We will miss you." But on the other side of her, a voice beckoned from those big lights beyond the city saying, "You don't have to stay. There are more flock for you to nurture and feed. Just look beyond your limits…look beyond the horizon."

"Oh my goodness, that was strange," Zera said. "I feel so blessed and thankful. But I'm not sure exactly what that meant. Am I supposed to be doing something else?"

"You know, Zera, that's hard for me to say. I think the Lord was showing you something! Maybe telling you that there is more to come."

"I think so," she said. "I'm not sure; I'll need to pray on that. I don't really know what that part of the dream meant for me."

"You'll find out eventually; I'm sure," I said.

"I guess you're right," Zera returned, and then she continued, "After I looked toward the horizon, all went black. Then I saw Max again. This time, I could see into his future! He had become very successful!" Zera took a deep breath. "In my dream, he had finally overcome his frustration and passed the state bar exam as well."

"Hallelujah!" I said.

After passing the bar exam, Zera saw Max opening his own private law office. He began to live the life that he had always imagined for himself. He was married, and he and his wife were a happy couple living in a beautiful and luxurious five-bedroom home. It was perfectly situated on three full acres of rural countryside right outside of a vast city. There were three luxury cars in the garage to match. Max and his wife also had two beautiful kids, twin girls in fact, who appeared to be approximately three years of age.

by Mrs. Patsy Bazile

Zera reached out to the girls in the dream and held their hands. She strolled with them in the front yard of Max's mansion while Max and his wife walked alongside them.

"I'm so happy you came to visit," Max mentioned to Zera in the dream.

Max's wife then said to Zera, "We are blessed to have you here, sister-in-law. Your faith has made your brother strong. We have learned so much from you."

Zera paused.

"It amazed me to see Max's life turn out that way in my dream! You know, in reality, I've only been to Max's home once. He's so far away, and I think he's gone so far just to get away from us…to get away from his family! When we were there, he seemed to be very uncomfortable with our presence."

"Why do you say that, Zera?" I asked.

"Max is such an angry person sometimes. He's always wanted a different life. Now it seems that he wants nothing to do with his family roots."

"That's so sad," I said. "I don't understand how he could have such ill feelings about your family, Mr. and Mrs. Faith especially. Your family is extremely blessed now."

"Today we are. But I don't think Max ever wants to acknowledge his humble hometown beginnings," Zera elaborated. "When we were at his home, we did not find out why we were there until he announced to all of his guests that he was getting married. Of course, we were happy for him, but at the same time, we felt horrible about the fact that he had not even bothered to introduce us to his new fiancé prior to that moment! To this day, he has not brought her here to visit us or anything."

"So that's why you never mention her," I said.

"Right," Zera confirmed. "I really don't know her."

"But in your dream you seemed to see how happy they had become."

"Yes. In my dream, it felt as if I really knew her. But, I've only seen her once. And as for his friends…well, at that announcement party, they were so rude and elitist. I may have said only ten words to that entire group of people over the course of the evening. Their conversation revolved around lofty topics that none of our family really were concerned with, except for Max, of course. Our blessings seemed to be of no interest to them because we did not fit into their picture-perfect, intellectual road to success. But that still wasn't our—the family's—main concern. We were still trying to get over the fact that we lacked so much information about Max's life and the woman he was marrying."

"I can only imagine how awkward that was," I said.

"Awkward is not the word. It's more like *flabbergasted*," Zera responded with a slight laugh. "But at least we left that night knowing that Max seemed to be in good hands. From what I recall, his fiancé was a psychiatrist. Maybe she has since pushed some sense into that head of his," Zera said. We both snickered.

And then I saw sadness well up in Zera's eyes.

"He has nothing to do with us anymore, but I still pray for him every day," Zera mentioned. "Everyone needs prayer. Everyone should know that someone loves them enough to pray for them, right?" she asked.

I smiled back and said, "That's for sure, Zera. We should all pray. We should pray for ourselves and for others. And I'm sure Max still knows that his family cares for him even though he chooses to distance himself from you all. Your prayers are not and will never be delivered to God in vain."

Upon making that statement, I was reminded that although Zera was a woman of faith, she still desired confirmation from another soul regarding her declarations and beliefs. I could see that this dream of hers was taking her to a new level in her relationship with God! I became anxious to know just how her dream would end, but I did not dare intercept what was being manifested by the Spirit!

"To be honest with you, I know," Zera responded. "I never feel as if I pray in vain. You know, Max barely has faith anymore from what I recall of him before he moved away. And I had not truly felt as if my faith could sustain him throughout all of the struggles he faced in his life. But this dream has done something for me! I now know in my heart that a breakthrough is on the way for him. My prayers shall be answered!"

"If you speak it, it shall be done," I said.

"It shall," Zera confirmed. "I know that just as my brother will be blessed, so shall my sister. But, well, this part of my dream was not so happy."

> *Aeria's adult life began to appear before Zera's eyes as Max's life faded away. She saw that Aeria was a settled woman, beyond her younger years when she had swayed back and forth according to any way life took her. Zera also saw that Aeria was less of a passive participant in her own life. She married a wealthy man able to keep her attention by constantly buying*

her beautiful clothes and expensive things. He lavished her with a luxury car, posh jewelry, leisurely trips, and live-in help that tended to all her needs. Aeria was living a fantastic life with her loving husband who was fourteen years her elder. And Zera saw two adorable children come into view, a daughter and son born to Aeria and her husband.

Zera stood by as Aeria walked over to her out of the scene in the dream. In her tight red dress, Aeria then said, "He is rich! That man can take care of me, free me from work, and give me the life I want. Look over there."

Upon that command from Aeria, Zera turned around and looked in the pointed out direction. She saw Aeria and her dream husband meeting for the first time in their mutual place of work. Zera could see that Aeria was a nursing assistant, and he was the chief operations officer of the health care facility. Zera could also see that it was not love at first sight.

"As time progresses, I will grow to love him, but this is not important to me now," Aeria whispered to Zera. She continued to look at herself in the dream sequence along with Zera.

"I just wanted a charmed life then. And I knew that he was the type of man who could love me always while I continue to live a care-free life."

Then a doorbell rang.

The scene disappeared, and Zera asked, "Where did that sound come from?"

"Oh, I think someone is at the door."

"What door?" Zera asked.

"That door," Aeria answered. Then a black door appeared in front of them, and Aeria opened it.

Two police officers stood there with black uniforms and pitch black sunglasses.

"We are sorry to inform you that your husband has been in a terrible accident," one of the officers said.

"He is at the hospital," the other officer added. "He is now in a coma, ma'am."

Aeria then broke down with tears streaming down her face. She fell to the floor, screaming and calling out to God!

"Oh my God! Oh my God! No! No! How can this be? How could you let this happen to me?"

"At that point, my dream became a nightmare," Zera said to me.

"My goodness, Zera," I said. "Sounds like that was an awful experience! Even though it was a dream, I bet it freaked you out! How could you deal with that?"

"Oh, I don't know," she replied. "But is was all God's doing. I guess that's why I wasn't awakened. I just kept on dreaming. Hold on. There's more."

At this point, my heart began to beat a little faster as I waited in anticipation for the words coming next as Zera continued to describe her dream to me.

Aeria found the strength to get up from her fall. Her red dress turned black, and a matching black hat with a very wide brim and sheer veil appeared on the top of her head. The veil darkened to completely cover her face, but huge diamond teardrops fell from under it to the black heels on her feet. She was weak, yet she found her way to a chair that appeared in an ornately decorated, but stark office. Aeria seemed to forget that Zera was nearby, thus Zera became a lone observer to all that was happening around them. In front of Aeria, a stout man appeared, sitting behind a huge desk piled high with paperwork. Zera knew that he was a lawyer, and she knew that he was there to add more horrible news to what she and Aeria were already privy.

"In the event of your husband's death, he has left a will, and I will present it to you," he said. The lawyer then adjusted the document in his hand and proceeded to read its contents.

"To my wife, Aeria, whom I've loved since I laid eyes on her, the woman whom I know did not love me the same way, I leave nothing, not even our house. Our house was not a home, and my love was not a wife. To my children I leave everything, and may they have mercy on her."

Aeria displayed a flustered expression. As she sat in her chair, her body and health instantly deteriorated. Zera saw Aeria's face sag and her body slump. She also saw that the black dress that Aeria wore transformed into tattered rags. The black hat that rested on her head morphed into a mangled web of disheveled hair.

Zera could feel raw emotion radiating from Aeria. She could sense Aeria's internal realization that she had taken her husband and children for granted. And just as she had chosen to focus on only herself and her desires, so did her children who

completely disowned her, yelling to her in the background, "Go! Go! We don't know you. Go away! Go away!"

White tiles began to materialize beneath Zera's chair. As she got up from her seat, beaten and battered by guilt, a face bowl and mirror appeared on an invisible wall in front of her. Aeria looked into that mirror, and she stared into her own regretful eyes. Then with a quick slice of her wrist with the razor that appeared in one of her hands, she fell backward and onto the ground.

"Dear God, please forgive me!" she begged. "This sin is despicable according to Your will. Almighty God please grant me a portion of my sister's faith so that my soul may still be saved. I must come to you. Oh Lord, this Earth is not my home anymore.

Zera leaned back in her chair and threw her hands up into the air.

"Thank you, Lord! The answer to my prayer was revealed!" she exclaimed.

I was amazed and profoundly moved by this reaction of hers.

"Yes, praise him!" I said, then I asked, "So your sister died in the dream?" I had to confirm what I had just heard.

"Yes, she did," Zera responded. "When I awoke from that dream, I felt my pillow soaked with tears and my forehead covered with beads of sweat! But this is what I know: My faith is as strong as steel, and my family depends on me for it!"

I realized that through all that Zera had experienced in her dream, she learned that God had anointed her with a special kind of faith, a faith that was more than sufficient for only her, and she was willing to share!

"You don't know how long I've been wanting to tell all of this to someone," Zera confided to me. "But I knew that I could not just tell anyone. It had to be someone special like you, another God loving and God fearing woman with strong faith as well. I wanted to tell my dream to you because I knew you would listen. You would not get bored from what I had to tell you, and you would never use my blessing as gossip or judgmental conversation with others."

"Oh, Zera. Of course not. I'm so thankful that you shared this experience of yours with me," I told Zera. "Listen, you don't have to worry about a thing. And I have been in awe, sitting here listening to you. It is undeniable: you have been chosen for a higher calling by the Lord, and He will be with you always. Your faith is confirmed!"

"I know," Zera said. "And I think that if this experience of mine can fit into your book in some way, please use it! We all have doubts and questions. And there are lots of answers to be uncovered.

For those of us who have faith, God makes his presence known! Perhaps someone can use my experience and learn from it. I trust that you will bring this to an audience who will benefit and learn from it."

"Absolutely," I said. "You came to me for a reason. This was meant to be. And for that reason, I know your experience will bless others when they read about it."

We both smiled, and then we looked around the restaurant.

"Folks are beginning to clear out," Zera said.

"Yes, they are."

"Let's get out of here, Sis," Zera said.

"Ok, if we must," I said. We both laughed because we were having a great time and did not want to leave. Nonetheless, we got up to go to our cars anyway.

§ § §

The Faithful Death

Over the next few weeks, I focused on organizing the content for my book. Because I was able to jot down excellent notes about Zera's dream during our conversation at the restaurant, I included it.

Before I knew it, three months had flown by. So, I made it a priority to call Zera one Friday evening after work. I figured she would perhaps be winding down from a long week as well. Her home phone rang and rang. No one was there. As a second resort, I then dialed her mobile phone number. I knew that Zera rarely answered her mobile phone on the first attempt to reach her, but I figured I would give it a go anyway. Still, no answer. Then, minutes later, I received a phone call. Zera's number appeared across my caller identification screen.

"Hello," I said.

"Hello," Zera responded. She took in deep breath. Then she released a lingering exhale.

"Hey, Zera, are you okay?" I asked.

"No. I'm on the road. Daddy is not well. I'm trying to get to my parent's house. I will have to call you back later. I gotta run, okay? We'll talk."

Click. Zera hung up the phone. That was so uncharacteristic of her. I did not dial her back. Instead, I decided that I would gather a change of clothes and a few personal care items for an impromptu trip to her parents' home. I knew that something was terribly wrong, and Zera deserved any help that I could offer her. Although I had previously intended on spending my weekend putting the final touches on the contents of my book, I told my fiancé that I had to go away for the weekend. Without question, the needs of my best friend took precedence over any of my other personal desires.

I arrived at Zera's parents' home about four and a half hours later. It was approximately 10:15 pm when I drove into the frontcourt of the beautiful Faith home. It was quite different from the one in that Zera grew up...the one that she recalled in her dream. This was because Mr. and Mrs. Faith had come a long way...on faith. Their current mansion was the result of hard work and blessings—the fruit of Mr. Faith's efforts to acquire a local farming hardware and equipment company that supplied products to a national farming corporation as well as local businesses.

Max was walking around outdoors. When he saw me he smiled, and then he approached my car. He walked up to me and gave me a big hug as I got out.

"Hey! W-What are you, uh, doing here?" he asked as he stumbled toward me. "I mean, it's so good to see you. Unexpected... but eh, you know. Come on in!"

It was quite obvious to me that Max had been drinking. I could smell the alcohol on his breath and in his clothes. Yet, I smiled back, and I pretended as if I had not noticed. Then I answered, "Well, I talked to Zera earlier this evening. She said that something was wrong with Mr. Faith. It sounded urgent, so I decided to drive up."

"Cool. Well, let's go in the house," Max said, haphazardly waving his arm toward the majestic front doors. He did not acknowledge that anything was wrong. Instead, he walked me into the beautiful Faith family home and through the grand foyer. He then pointed me to the huge family room.

"My mother is in there, lying down on the sofa," he said. He let me go on without him. I wondered why Max said nothing about his father, but I did not question him. I simply proceeded to the family room to meet "Momma Faith." That was my nickname for her because she always made me feel as if I were a part of the family every time I visited.

There was a lamp on the table next to the sofa, and it gently illuminated Momma Faith's silhouette. When she looked up and saw me, she smiled.

"Oh Lord, looks who's here," she said. "My goodness you drove all this way? How are you, sugar?" she asked me.

She reached out to me for a hug. I hugged her back and kissed her on the cheek.

"I'm doing fine, Momma Faith. I'm here because Zera mentioned to me that something came up with Mr. Faith. And it didn't sound good. What's going on?"

"Dear, I don't know," she said. "I just don't know!" Tears began to fall from her eyes. "My husband suddenly fell sick, so I called Zera. She drove down here, and as soon as she got here, she took Mr. Faith to her car, telling me she's headed to the hospital. She just sped off! And well, now, I haven't heard a word, not one word, from her yet! Something is wrong! I know it!" she said. "I know it! I just know it!" she continued with increasing intensity in her voice.

At that point, Max came stumbling into the room. I had gotten up to go to the kitchen and fetch Momma Faith a glass of water.

"Momma, just, uh, just try to stay calm!" Max said. "I'm sure Zera will be back soon! Hold tight."

When I went back into the family room, I handed the glass of water to Momma Faith. She took a sip.

"Yes, she will be back soon enough, I guess," Momma Faith said. "I will just lay here a while longer."

"Yes, ma'am. That's best," I told her. As Max turned around to go into the kitchen, I followed him. There were three hospitals in the region, so I asked Max which one had admitted his father.

"You know, I'm really not sure," he responded upon my inquiry. "I caught a last-minute flight down here after Momma told me to come. I'm just as lost as Mom is. She just told me that Zera took

Daddy to the hospital, and th-that's all I know. I'm sure it's all good. Daddy is in Zera's hands; and Zera knows best, right? It's all good."

I could see that Max was harboring some anger and discontentment with Zera. I was not surprised because Zera had mentioned this anger of his to me before. However, it also became apparent to me that Max and Mr. Faith were not close as well. I did not want to focus on that revelation just then, so I began making phone calls to the local hospitals. Sooner than expected, I located the emergency room that admitted Mr. Faith. I went into the room to tell Momma Faith that I had located Mr. Faith, but she appeared to be sleeping. Since I figured she needed to rest despite all of her worrying, I kept quiet as I grabbed my purse and keys. I dashed out the front door, and I saw that Max had already made his way to the porch again.

"Max, I located your father," I said to him.

"Ok," he responded. He took a swig of liquor upon acknowledging my comment.

"I'm headed to the hospital, do you want to come?" I asked.

"No, you—you go ahead," he said.

I did not quite know how to respond to Max's comment, so I simply said, "Oh, okay." I preceded to get into my car. As I settled into the driver's seat, I then figured it was best for Max to stay at home in his drunken condition. The hospital would perhaps not be so willing to understand his drunkenness at a time like this.

When I arrived at the hospital, I spotted the emergency room entrance and proceeded to drive into the parking lot.

"Thank you, Lord," I whispered as I found a convenient parking space near the entrance. I got out of my car, and I spotted Zera through a glass window of the emergency room waiting area. She spotted me as well as she was taking a seat. Instead of sitting, she ran out of the sliding glass doors and greeted me with open arms.

She could not say a word. All she could do was cry. We held on to each other as we walked into the waiting room, and then we both sat down. I did not say anything. I wanted Zera to regain her composure before speaking. Zera located a handkerchief in her purse, and she used it to wipe her face and dry her eyes.

"Oh, my goodness! I'm glad you came," she said. "I tried to pick up the phone and dial people several times to let them know what was going on, but I just couldn't. I didn't know where to start. I've been trying to keep it together. Dad is not doing well at all. There was no other option but to perform an emergency surgery. Daddy was going into cardiac arrest! I have been telling Momma that Daddy needs to take better care himself! This is just a whole lot for me to deal with!"

Zera began to cry again. "His health is fading, and he has not been seeing a doctor for the last few years. The company is growing, and he has been stressed. Now I don't know what to do! I'm just waiting and waiting now while Daddy lays there in surgery. My God! The Lord knows my heart and hears all my prayers. I'm praying so hard for Daddy right now!"

I started to speak, but before I could say anything, Zera wiped her tears again, and then asked, "Did you go to the house?"

"Yes," I answered. "Max is there, and I talked to Momma Faith. When I left, it looked as if she had fallen asleep. We had to calm her down a bit before I left. She's been worried, Zera. And I guess she just finally needed some rest."

"Oh Momma! I forgot! Do you see what I mean?" she asked as she looked at me and shook her head from side to side with disappointment. "I just left her at home. I remember her trying to get a hold of Max and Aeria. So Max made it? Why aren't they here with you?"

"What do you mean by 'they'? Him and Aeria?" I asked.

"Him and his wife," she clarified.

"I only saw Max."

Zera gave me a strange look of confusion. "Oh, okay," she said.

Then I continued, "Well, he told me to go on and get here without him?"

"What? Really? Why?"

"I'm not sure, Zera," I said. About a minute passed before I continued speaking. "And there is something else."

"Oh, gosh. What is it?"

"He seemed to be intoxicated," I revealed.

"Wow! That's so Max! He never thinks about his family. Here Daddy is in the hospital, and he's too intoxicated to come to the emergency room for him!" Zera fumed.

"Wait, Zera," I responded. "He was polite, it just looked like he had a lot on his mind. I don't know what it was, but he had to be drinking for a reason. Don't mind any of that right now. God's got it! Your brother is safe and sound with Mamma Faith, and God is with us."

Zera managed to muster up a smile. "You always know the right things to say to make people feel better," she said. "You were always very good at that."

I smiled as well and said, "That's what friends are for. They may not see or speak to each other every day. They may drift apart for a little while, but when there's a need to bring them back together, it always happens. That is how God works. He knows just who to place in our paths, and just the right time to put them there."

Zera then closed her eyes. She was tired as well. She quickly dozed off into slumber.

I began to pray for Zera's dad and the rest of the Faith family. Suddenly, I was overcome by a vision of letters taking form on the blank white wall in front of me. They appeared right there in the emergency room waiting area! I looked away briefly at a young couple who was in the waiting room with us, and it was obvious that they could not see it. Only I could see and read the following words:

> *"Zera is about to witness challenges that will weaken and attack the faith of those closest to her now. Relay to Zera this anointed message that was given to you by the Holy Spirit. Zera shall be the stronghold. Zera's faith shall be sufficient to recover and restore all."*

Instantly the words disappeared, and I knew what I had to do. I wondered when the right time would come for me to give the message to Zera. An urge suddenly came over me, and I felt as if there was no time to waste. So I walked up to the emergency room help desk, and I told the administrator that Zera and I would be sitting on a bench just outside the glass doors of the waiting area. I also asked her to let us know if the doctor comes out of surgery with any news concerning Mr. Faith. With just one tap on her shoulder, I woke Zera.

"Is it time to see the doctor?" she immediately asked.

"No. Not yet, but let's go get a little air."

She gave me a strange look, and she was a little reluctant to accommodate my request. However, she got up and came with me anyway. The urgency for me to relay the message from my vision to Zera stirred inside of me. I hastened to sit down and chat with her.

As we took our seat on the bench in the cool night air, I said to her, "Zera, I need for you to listen to me very carefully. The Spirit spoke to me. I have a message for you."

Zera sat up straight on the bench and said nothing. She just looked at me, very intently.

"The Lord has found favor in you…you and your faith. And it is your faith that has now been blessed with a more powerful anointing."

Zera's eyes glazed with water.

I continued, "It is your faith that will prove sufficient in helping others to see the light as it has already done in the past. But this time, there will be harder challenges coming. I don't know how to explain all of this, so please don't ask. But what I do know is that when the Holy Spirit tells us to do something, we must do it. You know this as well as I do."

Zera looked away from me and up to the stars. She had a very serious expression on her face, then it softened to reveal a smile. She began to speak.

"God really knows what He's doing doesn't He, my friend? He really knows how to reach us and let us know that it's Him. I have always known that there is something more He wants me to do. I just haven't known what it is. I'm still not sure, and I'm not even going to question it. But He could not have used a more convincing vessel."

I smiled.

"You," she said. "We are as close as blood sisters; and, of course, we are sisters in the name of Christ. I trust you. I know you would not steer me wrong. I guess we just have to see what happens from now on."

"Yes, that is what we must do," I said.

We got up and proceeded to walk back through the sliding doors of emergency room waiting area. But before we could get through them, the desk administrator called out to us.

"He's here," she said. "The doctor is coming out to speak with you, Miss Faith."

As the doctor approached us and looked into Zera's eyes, I knew that the news was not going to be good. I could see it in his reticent expression.

"Miss Faith," he said, as he inhaled and exhaled, "We did everything we could."

Zera brought her hands to her face. "Oh no!" she said. "My Daddy! Oh, no!"

The doctor touched Zera on her shoulder to comfort her. "I regret to inform you that he did not make it. I'm so sorry, Miss Faith."

As Zera sobbed, he rubbed her shoulder. He did not say another word. I leaned in to give Zera a hug to comfort her as well. After a few minutes, our consolation allowed Zera to settle into that upsetting moment. As she regained her composure, the doctor pulled a note out his pocket and handed it to her.

"Miss Faith, we found this note on Mr. Faith's back as he went into surgery," he said. He put the note in her hands, and then he said, "It will be okay." The doctor then looked over at me and nodded his head to bid me adieu. He backed away, and then he returned to the emergency room surgery area.

As I continued to stay close to Zera, she bawled, and she began to quote scripture, specifically Psalm 23:4 KJV.

"Yea, though I walk through the valley of the shadow of death, I will fear no evil: for thou art with me; thy rod and thy staff they comfort me," she said. Through all of her sobbing, she declared, "He wasn't afraid. I feel it. I know that my father was not afraid to leave us."

I responded with, "Amen." Then I proceeded to give her some space.

"I need to get the family together. Please call Momma's house, and find out if Aeria made it to town yet."

"Okay, I'll go do that now. Come and sit down, Zera," I said. I then guided her to the nearest waiting room seat. When she sat down, I found my mobile phone and dialed the phone number of the Faith family residence. It had gotten to be quite late, approximately 2:30 am. The phone rang a few times, but a female finally answered. Her voice sounded more youthful than that of Momma Faith.

"Hello," she answered.

"Hello. Aeria, is that you?" I asked.

"Yes, it's me. Who is this?" she asked.

I told her who I was, and she quickly remembered the sound of my voice.

"Hey! Yes, Mom just told me you were in town, and she didn't know where you were, but figured you caught up with Zera."

"Y—Yes, I did. I'm here with Zera."

"Good. How's Dad? Is everything alright?" she asked.

I could not answer Aeria. I just could not break the news to her…and tell her that Mr. Faith passed away. So I had an involuntary reaction to end the phone call. When I went back to Zera to mention that Aeria had made it to the family home, she handed me the note that the doctor had given her.

I read it, and I was shocked to learn that it had written on it the same bible verse that Zera quoted:

> *Yea, though I walk through the valley of the shadow of death, I will fear no evil: for thou art with me; thy rod and thy staff they comfort me (Psalm 23:4 KJV).*

I looked back at Zera. She displayed an odd, solemn smile on her face.

"Miss Faith, I'm here to escort you through the emergency room beyond the double doors. Are you ready to sign the release for your father's body?" a nurse gently asked after she walked up to us.

"Yes, I'm ready."

Zera appeared to be strong and ready to see her father. But just before she entered the double doors of the surgical area, she turned to look at me and say, "I told you he wasn't afraid. My daddy has never been afraid."

I simply smiled through all of my sadness as the double doors closed behind her. I wondered how she felt as she approached him. I figured that it was a difficult journey for her as she took those steps toward her father's lifeless body. Yet, I could tell that this was something that she had to do alone. So, I patiently waited for her to return, thinking that I may need to console her further after she took care of her procedural obligations.

Suddenly, the double doors flung open. Zera walked through them with what seemed to be more confidence than I had ever before witnessed in her. Through her sadness, she still wore a smile on her countenance, not an ordinary smile, but a smile of *reassurance and strength.*

"Let's go," Zera said. We began walking out of the hospital to our cars, "What a weekend this is turning out to be for you, huh?" Zera asked, looking down while shaking her head.

I responded, "I couldn't have come at a better time, Zera. Real friends do that for one another."

She perked up slightly. I got in my car; then, I waited for her to get into hers. When she exited the hospital parking lot, I followed her onward to the Faith home. We arrived there at about 5:00 am. The house was very quiet and dark. However, the lamp was still shining in the living room. We walked in. Momma Faith was awake, still lying on the sofa and blankly staring at the television, which depicted bouncing images. It was mute. Aeria was sitting in the recliner next to the sofa. Her eyes were closed, but I did not know if she was asleep or awake.

"Hi, Momma," Zera said.

Momma Faith sprang up as fast as she could. "Hey, baby. What happened? How's your Daddy?"

"Momma, where's Max?" Zera asked.

"He's in the guest room, Zera. Did you you hear me? How's your Daddy, I asked," Momma Faith said.

"Max," Zera called out. "Max?" She began walking to the downstairs guest room. When she walked in, Max was snoring very loudly.

"Max, wake up." She strongly nudged him, remembering that I had told her he was drunk earlier.

"Wh-What? What's going on?" he asked in a disoriented manner. As he opened his eyes, he noticed that Zera was standing over him. He rubbed his temple to relieve the thumping pain shooting through his skull.

"Zera? What's up? You're back from the hospital? Is Daddy back?"

Zera just looked at Max, and she tilted her head a bit. She looked at Max with disappointment. She was upset because her father passed; but she was also disappointed because Max was waking from a hangover. She could not come to terms with Max's actions and his careless behavior at such an important moment in time.

"Oh no, Zera. No…no…no…no. Don't tell me," he said. Max suddenly became flustered. He jumped up from the bed. "No one has to tell me a damn thing! He's gone, isn't he? I know he's gone! I already know it! And now it's too late!"

Zera reached out to Max, and he pushed her hands away. "No, no, can't you see? I am partly the blame! Daddy wanted me to change. He wanted me to come and see him more. He wanted to be a part of the family and the business, and now it's too late! I have to get out of here. I can't be here! I just cannot be here now!"

Max rushed out of the bedroom. I had made my way near the entrance of the bedroom when Zera went in to wake Max, so when he rushed by me, I tried to reach out to him as well. But I could not stop him.

"Where are my keys?" he exclaimed. "Where are my damn keys?" he yelled again.

No one answered Max. So he rambled around the kitchen until he found them. All of the commotion frightened Aeria.

"What is going on?" she asked, as she approached the kitchen. As I looked into her face, I could see that she had been crying.

"Max seems to have sobered up quite a bit since I was here earlier," I answered, making sure I was staying clear of Max's path. "Now he's upset, and I think he's about to leave."

"God help Max!" Zera spoke out in prayer. "I don't know where he's going but please be with him, Lord!"

"He will," I said to Zera, "He will." Then, slam! The front doors of the Faith house closed behind Max. Within seconds, he was in his luxury rental car, speeding out of the driveway.

Through all of this drama, Momma Faith had become frazzled, but she made her way into the kitchen where Aeria, Zera, and I were left looking at each other with bafflement.

"Hi, Zera," Aeria said. "My goodness, I did not even get the chance to say hello." Aeria then walked over to us and gave us hugs. "My two beautiful sisters, how are you?" Before we could answer, she then asked, "Is Dad okay?"

Zera quickly walked over to Momma Faith and grabbed her hand.

Quickly catching on to why Zera grabbed their mother's hand, Aeria then said, "Oh, no!"

"Momma," Zera said, feeling her mother's grip tighten around the width of her hand, "Daddy is no longer with us." Momma Faith grew weak, but Zera caught her. Momma Faith then let a hearty outcry, and the rest of us began to cry as well.

"Momma, Daddy is gone, but he was not afraid. I'm telling you, Momma. He was ready."

Through her tears, Aeria asked, "Did he suffer, Zera? Please tell me he didn't suffer!"

"Aeria, Daddy was strong. When I brought him to the hospital, he was in a lot of pain. But he tried his best to endure it. The next thing you know, they were taking him into surgery. There was no other way. Daddy knew. He knew he was leaving us. He was ready. Daddy is home in Heaven now."

"Let me go and sit down," Momma Faith said as she sniffled. "You girls. Come with me. Come with me and sit with me in the living room," she demanded.

We all followed her. This time, she sat in the recliner instead of on the sofa. Zera and I took our places on the sofa. Aeria dabbed her mother's tears away just before sitting on the loveseat. Minutes later Momma Faith began to speak.

"I should have known. My beautiful girls, I should not be surprised right now. A couple hours ago, throughout all my worrying about your father and what was going on with him, I had the most wonderful dream. I dreamed that I was escorted by an angel to the gates of Heaven, but he told me not to enter just yet. He told me to just stand there and wait on a visitor who would be coming along very soon. And I did not question him. I just nodded and stood there. I waited just like he wanted me to do. After that, I saw somebody's shadow in the distance, and it began to move toward me. I could not see the figure of the person casting the shadow because he was surrounded by a thick cloud. The cloud was as white as snow and as puffy as cotton. But as he got closer, the clouds around him thinned out. I could finally see him. It was the only man I'd ever fallen in love with, my dear husband, the loving father of my beautiful children."

Momma Faith then looked over at me. "In case he never told you, child, ever since you and my daughter became good friends, my husband has said time and time again that you were just like one of our own. He loved you dearly, and he was proud of you, too!"

I couldn't hold back the tears that began to run down my cheeks. All of us were still crying. However, Momma Faith was holding up exceptionally well.

Then Zera asked, "Momma, how are you handling this so well? Daddy is really gone. He's not coming back home."

by Mrs. Patsy Bazile

"Zera, do you really think that your father would have left this earth without telling me first? We talked about everything. There were never any secrets between us. And he loved the Lord...very much. God was the head of his life. Your father always said that the relationship he had with God came with the bonus of a special blessing he had asked for long ago. That blessing is related to two of his favorite scriptures about a husband and his wife."

Momma looked at me and said, "Hand me that Bible right there by the lamp."

I got the Bible and handed it to her. After receiving it in her hands, she took out a sheet of paper with some words written on it. She then handed that piece of paper back to me and asked, "Please read that for me, sugar. My husband wrote that."

I proceeded to read.

And they twain shall become one flesh; so then they are no more twain, but one flesh. (Mark 10:8 KJV)

Who findeth a wife, findeth a good thing, and obtained favour of the Lord. (Proverbs 18:22 KJV)

Thank You, Lord! And this request, I make unto thee, with all faith that is within my heart. Amen.

"Oh how awesome this is!" I thought as I raised my head to look at Zera and Aeria with pure surprise.

Then Momma Faith went on to say, "I must confess that I asked several times about this special request but he would always smile and say 'It's not a request anymore, it's a blessing, dear, and you'll know all about it when the time is right!' So, I eventually decided not to ask him anymore. We both had respect for each other's individual relationship with God."

Zera and Aeria began to cry aloud. Zera got up from the sofa and went to her mother's side. She sat on the arm of the recliner and placed her arm around her mother's neck for a warm embrace. Aeria stayed on the loveseat, but she leaned in to give her mother undivided attention. Momma Faith's voice was so soothing that it carried words that seemingly wiped our tears away.

"Girls, your Father confirmed the answer to his prayer tonight. He had already told me time and time again that he and I were one, just as God says. He told me that no matter where we were when God decided to separate us, He would allow my husband to tell me that he loved us all one more time. He did that in my dream. He told me not to worry because the Lord has called him home. And Zera, your father told me to tell you to trust in your special anointing. God has found favor in you. When he walked through that gate, girls, he said, 'God is with me, and God is with us all…always and forever. So do not be afraid of anything, not even death.' Now let me get some air," Momma

Faith said rising up from the recliner. "There is a beautiful sunrise coming up right now. I think I'll go to the patio and watch it."

§ § §

The Faithful Woes

The morning slipped into the midday hours. Zera contacted several out-of-town family members to inform them of Mr. Faith's passing. Because Max had not yet returned, Zera, Aeria and I all decided to leave the house and try to locate him by driving throughout the town. We had not made it out of the front courtyard driveway before Max drove up. He got out of that shiny car and walked up to us. He then apologized for his earlier behavior. He also officially announced to us that he and his wife separated due to his lack of attention toward her and his kids.

"She says I'm too focused on the wrong things in life, like status quo and way people view me. She says that I can't give my all to the family, if I don't give my all to myself first," Max said. "We just smiled and looked at him.

"Max, she's right," Zera said. "I don't know your wife, but she seems like a very smart woman."

"She is," he verified. Then with a light-hearted smile, he said, "Take your time, wherever you all are headed. Please be careful. I'm going to be here with Mom, and I'm not going anywhere so don't worry. Don't worry about anything."

Max sounded so sincere that there was no reason to doubt him, but the thing that amazed me the most was that, wherever Max had gone, he was completely sober, and not hung over any more. And he was beaming!

"Well, we don't have to go anywhere now, Max. We were about to try to find you," I said.

"I apologize for that too," he said. "I needed to get away for a bit, but I'm back now. So I guess you all don't need to worry about me anymore."

As I proceeded to get back out of my car, Zera said, "Hold on. I think I need to get out of the house now. Let's go. I haven't eaten anything since the middle of yesterday, and now I think I'm getting my appetite back."

"I'm getting hungry too," Aeria said. "Let's go. Let's go!"

"Ok," I responded. "We will go." I inspected Aeria's demeanor to figure out if she was having a mood swing because of her shouting. She seemed to be okay, so I said, "Max, we'll see you later, okay?"

"Sure," he said.

"All trust is in the Lord, so we trust Him with Max as well," Zera declared as she noticed my lagging concern.

"Uh, come on. Let's go…please! Please!" Aeria urged.

We all watched Max as he made his way into the house, then we got on the road, and headed to a nearby fast food restaurant. As I drove, I thought about the way that Max had said "Don't worry. Don't worry about anything." His words dangled in the back of my mind, and I wondered what unspoken particulars were behind them.

We purchased our meals and ate them there at the restaurant. We spent quite a bit of time there, because there was no reason for us to rush. We talked only a little between solemn pauses as others around us went about their normal activities. Then we drove back to the Faith family home. Momma Faith had returned to her favorite resting place, and she was sleeping on the sofa again. I could hear Max snoring in the downstairs guest room again as well. Evening was creeping upon us and we all had gotten very little sleep the night before, so we took our showers. Zera, Aeria and I then went to the upstairs bedrooms to get some rest.

After I said my prayers, I lay in bed thinking of Aeria. Upon initially seeing her again, she seemed to be her normal self. However, as time progressed throughout the day, she became unusually quiet. In the last couple of hours before we all went to bed, she began entering a trance and offering childlike monosyllabic responses when Zera and I talked to her. My thought did not linger because I was very tired. Sleep shortly took over me.

The next morning, we all got up at around the same time. We woke up to clanking of pots and pans. As we all found our way to the kitchen, we joined Momma Faith who was humming a church hymn and making breakfast. Her eyes were slightly blood-shot, so I could tell that she had tossed and turned throughout her sleep-deprived night, but she still smiled and said, "I thought we'd all sit and have a good breakfast before going to the mortuary. We must nourish our bodies, and God will nourish our souls."

Zera and I in unison said "Amen."

Go ahead, and fix yourselves a plate," Mrs. Faith said. "Where is M—?"

Before she could finish asking her question, the kitchen door opened. Max walked in, fully dressed.

"Hey, Momma," he said. He went straight to her and kissed her on the cheek. "Thanks for breakfast." He joined us as we piled food on our plates, and then he sat with us at the breakfast nook.

No one asked where he had gone, and Max did not volunteer any information. We simply enjoyed our breakfast, and ate peacefully. After eating breakfast, Zera and Aeria washed the dishes. Momma

Faith got an early start on getting dressed for our visit to the mortuary. I was the first to finish getting ready. Zera and Aeria were the last. As we headed toward the door to leave, Max announced to us that he had some business to take care of. Momma Faith looked at him with suspicious eyes, but she did not respond to his announcement. She simply proceeded to walk out of the door with the rest of us.

"I will see you all when you get back," he said as we left. Only Momma Faith responded.

"See you later, son."

When we arrived at the mortuary, the funeral director greeted us at the door.

Momma Faith looked at him, and said, "Well, first things first."

"Yes, ma'am," he responded, knowing exactly what she meant. He then escorted us toward the rear of the facility so that we could see Mr. Faith. Zera and Aeria both attempted to go with Mrs. Faith, but she stopped them.

"I must do this by myself, girls," Momma Faith said. "I know your father has something else to reveal to me. I will be fine. Just wait here."

She smiled and went on with the funeral director to the back room. We stood there in silence, just looking at each other for a moment. Then Aeria broke her silence.

"What does Momma mean? What does she mean by Daddy has something else for her? What does that mean?" she asked while fidgeting and looking all around as if she did not know what to do next.

Zera reached out to Aeria and grabbed her hand. "Momma is going to be okay, Aeria. You know how close they were. She's okay, Aeria, and we will all be alright too. God will see to that because He's already promised that to us. Remember Psalm 34:18 (NKJV). Remember it tells us that 'The Lord is near to those who have a broken heart, and saves such as have a contrite spirit'."

Zera then paused. Aeria still appeared to be bewildered. A strange silence engulfed the room; and, I heard a voice speak to me.

"Zera's way has been established by the Lord, for she is now anointed for her higher calling. Speak not of this now, for you will know when the time is right. And know that the Lord has found favor in you as well."

Then the squealing double doors broke the silence as Momma Faith returned from seeing her husband.

"Okay, girls," she said. "Let's go into the office to start preparing the arrangements."

"I'll stay in the foyer," I said. I figured this was a special moment for only Momma Faith and her daughters to focus on while honoring Mr. Faith's life as well as possible. Aeria turned down the offer to assist Zera and her mother with making arrangements as well. She seemed extremely relieved to join me in staying behind.

Immediately after Momma Faith and Zera went into the office, Aeria burst into tears. I guided her to a seat, and we sat down together.

Releasing words between gasping moments of sorrow, she said, "I don't know if I can take all of this! I'm not that strong! I—I don't know how to deal with this!" She then laid her head on my shoulder.

"Let all of your pain go," I said.

I consoled her. My heart ached, and I could feel her agony. If Aeria could have grown wings and taken flight to get away, I knew that she would have surely done so in that moment. I prayed a silent prayer for her. "Touch Aeria now, oh, Lord. Please touch her," I pleaded. "Mend her broken heart and save her crushed soul."

We sat in silence as we waited, and I meditated on my plea to God to help Aeria and the rest of the Faith family in this time of need.

After quite some time had passed, the funeral director's door opened, and Momma Faith and Zera came out toward us.

"The funeral will be next weekend," Zera stated. "This should give our family and friends enough time to get here for the services. Everything will take place on the same day."

"Your father would have wanted it this way," Momma Faith continued. "And there was nothing for us to really do but execute his wishes. So there…it's done." As the words escaped her lips, they sailed on short breaths of relief—as if a heavy burden was lifted from Momma Faith's body.

Aeria went to her mother and hugged her. Together, they began walking toward the car. But Zera and I slowly trailed them. When Zera figured that her sister and mother could not hear us, she said, "Remember when you lost your father, and I said, 'I can't say that I know how you feel, but my heart aches for you because I can only imagine'?"

"Yes, I do," I recalled.

"Well, now I know. I know exactly how you felt. I'm feeling it right now, and I'm hurting really bad! But you know what?"

"What, Zera?" I kindly questioned.

by Mrs. Patsy Bazile

"My heart is glad because your message to me from the Holy Spirit has been confirmed. While we were talking to the funeral director, trying to pay attention to all of the details that he needed to discuss with us, I had a strange experience. A cool breeze came over me, and I rubbed my arms. No one else in the room felt it. Then someone spoke to me! The funeral director just kept on talking, as if nothing was going on, but I could hear this other voice. 'And he said unto me, my grace is sufficient for thee: for my strength is made perfect in weakness. Most gladly therefore will I rather glory in my infirmities, that the power of Christ may rest upon me (2 Corinthians 12:9 KJV).' Those were the words spoken by that voice."

Zera and I hugged each other, and we gave all glory to God. We then joined Momma Faith and Aeria in the car. When we got back to the Faith family estate, Max was working in the front courtyard manicuring the hedges.

"God, help Max. He has to cope in his own way," Momma Faith said. "We have lawn maintenance folks to help us with that."

A tear fell as Aeria quickly said, "He'll be okay, Momma."

After we all walked into the house, I brewed some tea for us. I offered Zera a moment to sit and talk for a little while because the weekend was ending. My fiancé had already been calling me to make sure that everything was going okay. Additionally, I needed to go back home to the city to take care of some of my responsibilities before coming back the following weekend. Zera and I talked under the canopy that covered the rear patio of the Faith mansion. She assured me that she would be okay as she finished handling the funeral preparation activities. She once again graciously thanked me for being there for her as well. With the offer of a late lunch, she tried to get me to stay longer, but I had to decline. I wanted to get back home at a decent hour, so I left before nightfall. As I traveled back to my residence, I thanked God for the beautiful and clear passing day. There was very little traffic on the highway, and my fiancé kept me alert with his phone calls to make sure that my travels were going well.

When I got back to my house, I felt good. I was ready to relax, but thoughts of Zera and her family stayed on my mind.

"What a time…what a time," I thought to myself. I lifted the Faith family up in prayer, and my thoughts gave way to a deep, sleepy night.

By the time Wednesday came around, I had purchased a beautiful black dress to wear to the funeral. I wished that I had purchased it for a different occasion, but I adored it just the same. I was happy that my week was progressing well, and I had succeeded in catching up on all of the tasks that I had planned to complete. Thus, by the time Thursday arrived, I was able to get in bed early, and enjoy watching the late night news after I said my prayers.

When I got in bed, the phone rang. It was Zera.

"Hey! So sorry to call you this late. Is this okay?" she asked.

"Zera? Yes, it's fine. It's not too late. Actually it is sort of early for me given all of the stuff I have going on. How are you? Is everything okay?"

"Well, Aeria's husband called about an hour ago. He told me that she had been acting strangely ever since she got back home. Today, she started grabbing some of her things and piling them up at the front door, saying that she was coming back to Momma's house!"

"What?" I asked in a state of excitement tinged with confusion.

"Yes! He said she then started yelling at the kids for no reason, telling them to leave her alone. When he asked her to calm down, she lashed out at him and the kids, waving her arms and fists like a mad woman!"

"Oh, my God, Zera! What was wrong with her?" I asked.

"Well, I—I don't know!" Zera continued. "He said she was yelling at him too saying, 'As for God, He knew I couldn't take this! He knew it, and He did it anyway! What kind of God does that?' He said she then changed like night and day! She went from frowning and yelling to, all of a sudden, laughing. Then she ran out of the house barefoot with some of her items in her hands!"

"Zera, it sounds like Aeria snapped. Oh my goodness! God help her!"

"The kids were crying because they were shocked. I'm sure they have never seen Aeria act like that before. Derrick tried to calm them down before walking out of the house to see where she was going. When he went after her, he caught a glimpse of her turning the corner. So he grabbed the kids and put them in the car. He then drove in the direction that he last saw her. He caught another glimpse of her at the next corner, but when he got there, she vanished into the darkness!"

"Dear God! Oh Lord!" I exclaimed.

"He says he called the authorities and we, we—we haven't heard…"

At that point, I could hear Max calling for Zera in the background.

"I'll have to call you back," Zera said. She abruptly ended our phone call.

There was no sleeping for me now. I got up and started praying again. I went into my living room and sat in my recliner. I stared at the television, paying no attention at all to what was playing on it. Two hours had gone by, and then the phone rang once again. I took a deep breath before answering.

"Hello", I said.

"They found Aeria! She was hit by a car! Physically...she was not badly injured."

"Oooh! Praise God!" I said. "Where is she now?"

"Derrick told me that they are still in the hospital. She's not in any condition to leave."

"What do you mean?" I asked. "I thought you said that she was not badly injured."

"Well, she doesn't know her name. She doesn't know her husband, the kids, me, Momma, or Max! When Derrick put the phone to her ear, and I said hello, Aeria didn't know what to say to me! She didn't know me!"

"Oh no!" I said. "I can't believe this."

"I know," Zera said. "This is a lot to deal with right after Daddy's death. Oh my God! I have to have faith. I have to be strong. The Lord is going to make everything all right. I—I know he will!"

"Yes, Zera, He will," I confirmed.

"I just have to keep in my mind that there is a lesson to be learned from everything that God does. I just know it, and I cannot lose hope. The doctor said that Aeria needs to be admitted to a medical center for mental trauma patients. He thinks she is suffering from a nervous breakdown, and the accident didn't help."

"Okay. I think Aeria will likely need to undergo some extensive rehabilitation. Just hang in there. The important thing to remember is that Aeria walked away from that accident with her life. She's still here with us," I offered with optimism.

"You're right. You're absolutely right," Zera said. She took a deep breath. "When I asked Momma how she felt about Aeria being placed in a medical facility, guess what she said?"

"What? I hope Momma Faith is holding up okay," I responded.

"She is," Zera reassured me. "Momma said it doesn't matter how she feels about it. What matters now is what is best for Aeria. She said that we all just need to make sure that Aeria gets all the earthly help she needs! God and *her husband* will do the rest!"

"God and *her husband*, as in *Mr. Faith*? That's interesting," I said.

"I know," Zera responded. Then there was a few seconds of silence between us.

Afterwards, I continued, "Well, I'm glad Momma Faith is staying focused on the Lord in these trying times. But what about you, Zera? How do you feel?"

"Hmm. You know it's the strangest thing. My old faith would have been *broken* or *unsettled* by now. Honestly, I know I would be questioning God! But my *new faith* has allowed me to look beyond what is happening now. I feel just like Momma. I know that God is up to something!"

"Zera just remember this: But God is faithful, who will not suffer you to be tempted above that ye are able; but will with the temptation also make a way to escape, that ye may be able to bear it (1 Corinthians 10:13 KJV)," I said. "You will get through this."

"I know I will. This too shall pass," she said. "The sad thing is that Momma and I will not be able to be there when Aeria is admitted to the facility. It's okay though, I said a prayer with Derrick over the phone. He told me that it helped, and he says he will take care of everything. He's still going to try to make it to Daddy's funeral. Momma and I are looking forward to seeing the kids again."

"That's good. I will pray for him too," I said.

"Thank you. We appreciate that. Well, it's getting late. I'll let you go," Zera concluded. "We'll talk soon, okay?"

"Okay," I said.

"Goodnight."

"Goodnight."

I looked over at the clock. It was 2:45 am. Finally, on this Thursday morning, my eyelids were getting heavy. "Thank goodness I took off today," I thought to myself. I took a few minutes to think about the errands I needed to run and chores I would need to finish before making my trip to Zera's hometown again. Just when I got a handle on how I thought my day would unfold, I dozed off confidently knowing that everything would be okay.

§ § §

The Faithful Funeral

On Saturday morning, I got out of bed before dawn. "Thank you, God, for waking me up this morning and starting me on my way!" I said. Then, I continued to pray in silence, giving glory to God and His infinite power to protect His flock. After eating a blueberry waffle, I took a shower and got dressed. By 7:00 am, I was heading to the Faith family manor on that beautiful, bright morning.

My timing was excellent. When I got to the mortuary, the ushers at the entrance were about to close the doors to the visitation area. Pastor Gabriel was preparing to preside over the visitation services. When I walked in, Max was one of the first people I recognized. His eyes were bloodshot red. But he still managed to smile at me when he saw me too. He came over to me and gave me a hug and a kiss on the cheek. He then escorted me to a reserved seat. I was touched. If ever there had been any doubt in my mind about the Faiths' regard for me as family, it would have been vanquished right then. As I sat down, I greeted Momma Faith with a touch on her shoulder. She placed her hand on mine and smiled. "I prayed that God would get you here safely," she said.

Zera chimed in. "I knew that He would!" She smiled at me as well, and then she turned her attention to the pastor. He was taking his place in front of the crowd behind a podium.

The viewing ceremony began with "This Little Light of Mine" as the opening song selection. One of the deacons from the New Beginnings Church of Christ then read the following scripture: The Lord is near to those who have a broken heart, and saves such as have a contrite spirit (Psalm 34:18 NKJV). Afterward, a deaconess led the congregation in a holy chant. Then the Pastor stood for remarks for the short program before reading Psalm 23, verses 1 through 6.

He read, "The Lord is my shepherd, I shall not want. He makes me lie down in green pastures; He leads me beside the still waters, He restores my soul…"

My mind drifted. I thought about Aeria, who was unable to be there because of her accident and admission to the mental trauma facility. My mood became glum, and Zera turned to me. It was as if she was reading my mind. She mouthed to me, "She's okay. She, Daddy, and God are all here." I was stunned into a better mood as I smiled and refocused on the Pastor.

After the pastor's message, Zera, Max, and I viewed Mr. Faith's body for the last time. Momma Faith sat in her seat quietly. Zera motioned for her to join us, but she remained seated. She remained calm as well with a reassuring demeanor.

"Our time was very special. We've already said our goodbyes for now," Momma Faith said.

No one else said a word. We simply bid our final farewell to Mr. Faith, and then we prepared ourselves for the burial.

When we arrived at the church cemetery, the grounds were already crowded with friends, family, and other community members. This was no surprise to me because the Faith family were well known and highly regarded in their town. All of the surroundings were nicely prepared. Flowers were displayed everywhere. There was a mass choir consisting of not only the church's men's, women's, and youth ministries, but also family members and friends. After the choir sang their well-rehearsed selections, Mrs. Faith received a tribute from the board of deacons and their wives. It was a large portrait displaying both her and her husband seated hand in hand. An ornate gold frame surrounded the image, which captured a moment in time in the recent past. Mr. Faith was honored with beautiful, kind words from various organizational representatives and business committee members who had the opportunity to work with him. The pastor's message was divine, as it elaborated on his Psalm 23 inspiration, offered during the visitation ceremony at the mortuary. As Pastor Gabriel delivered his message, he paused several times to regain his composure, because he thought about how much Mr. Faith remained committed to God, his family, the church, and the total community as well.

When it was time to begin lowering the body of Mr. Faith in his grave, Mrs. Faith was not ready. She got up, and walked over to the casket. She motioned for the pause of the lowering. Tears began to fall, and she asked one of the pallbearers to open the casket for one last time. Momma Faith then looked over at the pastor and said, "I just have to give him one last kiss. It was here at this church that your father united us in matrimony."

He nodded his head, and said, "Yes, ma'am."

When the pallbearer opened the casket, Momma Faith leaned over to kiss her husband.

"There," Momma Faith said. Then, she walked back over to her seat. Max stood up to embrace her. The pastor then motioned for everyone to stand as the lowering of Mr. Faith's body resumed. Onlookers stared in bereavement to reconcile the fact that this upstanding pillar of the committee was finished with his mortal labor.

Most funeral attendees gathered at the Faith family residence for the repass. Zera and I had not gotten a chance to sit and talk since my arrival because of everything that was going on, but everyone else that I met still treated me like family. Yet, at the first opportunity that I found to escape the crowd and the mournful mentions, I walked over to a bench located at a secluded portion of the estate. A large shade tree near the small pond accentuating the Faith family manor covered that bench. Still, Max spotted me going there, and he soon met me there. In his hands he brought glasses of lemonade.

"I've really grown to love lemonade," he declared. "I thought I'd bring you some too. Enjoy."

I kindly took one of the glasses from him, but before I could say anything, he started walking away.

"Max," I said. "Are you okay? I was about to thank you for the lemonade."

"Oh. Yes. I'm fine. I will see you all a little later. I'm thinking the crowd will thin out soon, so I think I'll get away for a bit," he responded.

I sat down and enjoyed the gentle breeze in the shade of the tree. The lemonade was cool and refreshing, one hundred percent natural, and tastier than any mixed powder beverage or canned lemonade that any company could sell me. Soon Zera discovered where I was as well, and she came over to talk to me.

"Hey, Lady!" she said. "What are you doing way over here?" she asked.

"I just needed a little quiet time. How are you holding up?" I asked.

"As well as can be," Zera said. She glowed, and offered me one of the most graceful and serene expressions of strength I have ever witnessed.

"That's good, Zera," I said. Then I asked, "Have you heard anything about what's going on with Aeria?"

"Well, I just talked to Derrick. He says that no one can visit her for at least thirty days. The doctor has informed him that in the event of an emergency, he will be the first to be notified."

"I see," I said. "That's rough not being able to communicate with your sister for so long."

"Yes. It is; but it will be fine. I know that her condition is going to get better! The Holy Spirit has confirmed this for me. God told me so. Right there in the kitchen at Momma's house, He did! Late last night, as I mentally prepared myself for today while cleaning up the kitchen, I heard a voice. 'Do not fret for Aeria!' it said to me. 'Your faith is sufficient, and her mind will be let free while she is born again in Christ. Your dream of that life that she could suffer has been realized within her as well! She now knows the significance of both her life and her death.'"

"Glory to God!" I shouted. "I am so happy to hear this, Zera!"

We gave each other a big hug. I grew confident from every one of Zera's uplifting words received by the Lord.

"That makes me feel a whole lot better. Of course, I will still be here until Monday morning, because I am here to help. But it sure is good to know that God's grace is comforting us," I said.

"Yes, it is. And that's great," Zera replied. "But before you leave, I'll take you to lunch. 'No' is not an option no matter what food is left over in the house, okay?"

"You got it!"

We stayed by the pond a little while longer throwing rocks into it to pass time. Then Zera asked, "Are you ready to go back in the house? I think the crowd is just about gone."

"Sure," I said.

After we walked back into the house, we noticed the untidiness that resulted from the repass activities. We began getting the house back into pristine condition. Shortly thereafter, Max walked in. Just as he had promised, his return was contingent on the crowd dissipating. When he arrived, he greeted us. Then, he found Momma Faith who was sitting on the patio with a snack.

"Hey, Mom, I'm back," he said.

She looked at him and said, "You know, Max, you're going to be okay."

Max kissed his mother on the cheek and said, "There was a time I would have never said this, but now I know that's for sure, Mom. I know I will."

As we cleaned the living room, we could hear their conversation. Hearing Max's self-assured words, Zera whispered to me, "God is good! God is so good!"

I whispered back, "Yes. He is."

Max then retreated to one of the upstairs guestrooms, opposed to the one downstairs.

As Zera and I finished tidying the house, we grew tired. Momma Faith seemed to still be wide-awake, but when she realized that we were tired, she said, "Try to get some rest, girls. And don't worry about me; I won't be too far behind you."

We then gave her a good night kiss, and like children, we went upstairs to our respective bedrooms. Completely wiped out from a day of travel and taking part in the funeral ceremonies and clean up duties, I knew that sleep would come very easy for me that night. As soon as my head hit the pillow, I fell asleep. I had one of the best night's rest ever.

The next morning, Momma Faith insisted that Zera and I go to Sunday church service although she would be staying home. Zera and I got dressed, and as Zera grabbed her car keys, we heard Max coming downstairs.

"Uh, where do you two think you two are going without me?" Max asked as he hurried down.

"Oh, look at our lovely children!" Momma Faith said, as if she were speaking to someone else—Mr. Faith perhaps. She went on to say, "Have a blessed time, and take care of those girls, my son!"

"Will do, Momma," Max said. "I'll be driving."

After Max's announcement, Zera hung her keys back on the key rack. Then we all walked out of the house and got into the luxury sedan that Max rented so that we could get to morning church service. The choir sang praises to the Lord. Pastor Gabriel gave us a marvelous sermon. However, what surprised me most about that day was Max's decision to dedicate his life to God! When the doors of the church opened, Max threw his hands in the air and testified before God, "I'm coming home!"

"My dad and my Father up in Heaven have helped me to find my way in this world!" he exclaimed.

When he made his way up the aisle to stand before Pastor Gabriel for acknowledgement, Zera and I burst with excitement and tears of joy. Those same tears of joy outpoured again when we later brought the exhilarating news to Momma Faith. Pastor Gabriel joined all of us later at the Faith estate to fully express his joy. We sat around the family room table while Pastor Gabriel gleamed expressions of pride and joy.

"Mr. Faith was such an upstanding man in the church. You have some big shoes to fill there, son. But you are your father's son. And I know that you will make him smile from Heaven," Pastor Gabriel said to Max.

"Yes, sir, I will," Max said.

"I know that you haven't told your family this, but I think I should share this with them Brother Faith. Do you mind?" the pastor asked.

"No, go right ahead. I'm ready."

"Well, you see, family, Brother Max has been coming to see me ever since he got in town. He told me about the separation with his wife, and the fact that she wanted to take the kids away from him. Brother Max told me that he was chasing frivolous dreams and friends who did not really care for him…they only cared about what he could do for them or how good he could make them look. Well, see, I even know that Brother Max was beginning to lean on alcohol to help him cope with fitting into a group of people that he really didn't identify with."

"My Lord," Momma Faith interjected.

"But it's okay, Mrs. Faith. "It's all good because God has now stepped in. *He* has intervened!"

"Thank you, Lord," we all said.

"Brother Max has even been reconciling with his wife. They have been talking on the cell phone, trying to patch things up, isn't that right, Brother Max?"

"Yes, sir, that's right!"

"So, Mrs. Faith, it's all about joy right now in the calm of the storm. I have to ask, is there anything special that I can do for you to celebrate this joyful occasion?" Pastor Gabriel asked.

Momma Faith looked at Max. Max remained silent, wondering what his mother would say next.

"Pastor, thank you so much," she answered. "But believe me, Max is already blessed! Now he is not only celebrating with us—he's also celebrating a life with God! That's as special as it gets!"

"Amen!" we all chimed.

Then Pastor Gabriel said, "You are absolutely right, Mrs. Faith. You are truly a woman of God." He then went on to quote a scripture from the bible saying, "As for God, His way is perfect; the word of the Lord is tried, he is a buckler to all those who trust Him (Psalm 18:30 KJV)."

Upon leaving the Faith home, Pastor Gabriel shook hands with Max, and said goodnight to everyone. Max walked with the pastor to his car, and when he came back into the house, he was still smiling.

We stayed up and talked late into the night. All of the Faiths reminisced about all of the good times they had with Mr. Faith. They also recalled the moments when he demonstrated profound strength for protecting the family, the home, and acquiring the quality of life that they all benefitted from. They were happy to share with me stories about past moments that amazed me and gave me a true picture of how dedicated Mr. Faith was to God.

Monday morning came surprisingly fast, and I was happy to sleep in late. By the time I got myself together and headed downstairs, I heard singing in the kitchen. Momma Faith and Zera were singing hymns while they were cooking breakfast, and they sounded spectacular!

"Amen! Amen!" I said, as I approached.

As they finished the hymn, I asked, "Is there anything that you two need help with?"

"Help? No, sleepy head!" Momma Faith said with a brilliant smile. "Umm hmmm, you got here just in time. You ain't fooling nobody," she heckled with a hearty laugh. "Just come on here and fix your plate. The food is all cooked for you, so you can at least fix your own plate."

I was overjoyed to see Momma Faith so happy. I laughed.

"Yes, ma'am. I will surely fix my plate."

As I made my way past them, Zera laughed as well.

"But don't eat too much though, because we still need to do lunch at eleven!" Zera reminded me.

"I haven't forgotten, Zera," I said, still tickled by Momma Faith's jeering.

"Okay," she responded.

Breakfast was fantastic! Momma Faith's cooking never disappointed me. After eating, I enjoyed as much of the Monday morning as I could by sitting and talking to her and Zera. It felt good being there with them, opposed to doing normal Monday morning tasks in the office. After I talked to them, I packed my belongings and brought them downstairs. I stowed them in the coat closet in the foyer so that I could easily get to them when I was ready to go back home. When 11:00 am approached, Zera punctually asked if I was ready for lunch. I confirmed, and we got in her car to go to the mom and pop Italian restaurant at the town limits along the interstate highway. There, the food was amazing as well. I could taste the authenticity and richness poured into it. Zera and I stuffed ourselves until we could eat no more. When we regained our strength and found it possible to move again, Zera attempted to delay my departure just as she did during the prior weekend.

"Come on, let's go to that new outlet mall right up the highway." She said.

"Zera, how far is it?" I asked.

"Just about five miles. That's it," she informed me.

I had to refuse. I needed to stick to my schedule, and I knew that a trip to the mall would set me back by at least an hour. I also knew that Zera simply cherished our friendship, so I wanted to make sure she understood why I declined.

"Well, Zera, there is no other place I'd rather be right now than with you and the family; but my life awaits in full swing back in the city. You know how that is," I said. "You will be fine. I know you will. And when you get back to the city, we need to do better at staying in contact with one another."

"We do, and we will," she said. She then motioned for the waiter to bring the check while saying to me, "I will keep you posted about Aeria too."

"Are you reading my mind again?" I asked.

"No, but I know you, remember?"

I laughed. She did too. After she paid our lunch bill, we headed back to the Faith family estate. By the time we made it back, Momma Faith had packed all sorts of food for me to take back home.

"Oh, my goodness! I won't have to cook for a month!"

She smiled and said, "Well, you can share some with your friends and co-workers!"

"I'll see. Knowing how good it is, I may not be able to do that!"

We all erupted with laughter.

After I filled my car to capacity, I gave Momma Faith, Zera, and Aeria's children huge hugs. I noticed that Max was gone, so I said, "Where is Max?"

"He's at church," Momma Faith said. "I think that boy has really turned a new leaf in life. He's in a meeting with Pastor Gabriel. He told me that they have a lot of business to discuss."

"Oh, wow!" I said.

"Tell me about it," Zera said. "My brother is suddenly really interested in things going on back here at home now. It's all so new to us."

"Yes, and that is a blessing. Tell Max I said I'm sorry he wasn't here when I left. Let him know that I wish him the very best!" I told everyone.

As soon as everyone said okay, I got into my car, cranked the engine, and got on the road. It was by pure luck that I stopped at a gas station and spotted Max driving up behind me. As I got out of my car, he came toward me with a huge grin. He swiftly picked me up and whirled me around!

"You be careful and call us when you get back home! That's an order, okay?" he said. He made sure that I landed perfectly on my feet.

I was grinning as well, but I was wondering what had gotten into him.

"I will, Max," I said, and then I cleared my throat to prepare myself to ask him the next question I had.

"Um, well, uh, have you been…"

I did not need to finish asking my question because he asked it for me.

"Have I been drinking? That's it, right? That's what you were going to ask me, right?" Max cleverly questioned.

"Well, yes. I'm just concerned. Have you been okay? Your dad, and now Aeria...I know all of this has been rough on the family," I said.

"You know what? It has; but I haven't had a drink since God allowed Dad to come and see me."

I tilted my head a bit in confusion, and I listened intently to what Max had to say next.

"It was me all along," he continued. "I have mistreated those closest to me, and I have had no regard for family. I was blind and now—thank God—I see! I am very successful, but I have never really been thankful for it all. And it has been tearing me up inside to keep up appearances—getting what I want out of life, but running over people while I do it. Zera, I only turned to alcohol because I was trying to cover up how I felt like trash inside. I have been really foul to people, and my wife had been trying to get me to see that. I finally see it now!"

"Oh, Lord, Max, I had no idea," I said.

"There is so much that I have to share with Mom. Pastor Gabriel has taken me under his wing as my spiritual advisor. The Holy

Spirit has made me free, and Daddy said God has a special mission in store for me!"

I nodded my head, and said, "Amen, Max."

"I even know about Zera's higher calling and anointing. I know that her faith is helping us to get through this tough time. As for Aeria, she'll be fine as well. God has a plan for her," Max concluded.

Tears welled up in Max's eyes. He smiled as he noticed my tears form as well. Max then kissed me on the cheek and said, "Now get in your car and go home so that you're not on the road too late! And thank you for being a part of our family. You know we love you."

After he spoke those words, I could not say anything else. I got into my car as he commanded, and I drove off. I was a mess of emotions, feeling happy and sad at the same time. Yet, I also felt blessed! It was another beautiful day, and as I took to the highway. I listened to my gospel CD, and I thought about various events that took place during my visits with the family…the sadness, the joy, the restoration and rebirth of faith, and so on. I was especially relieved to witness a new strength and love for God that took over Max. As I thought of all of these things, a scripture came to mind:

> *Be strong and of good courage, do not fear nor be afraid of them; for the Lord your God, He is the One who goes with you. He will not leave you nor forsake you (Deuteronomy 31:6 NKJV)*

"God, thank you for loving us all!" I shouted in the car. I continued to bask in blessed assurance as I continued my journey.

After getting back home, I unpacked my belongings along with the mounds of food items I brought back with me. I also called my fiancé to tell him that I safely made it back home.

"How is the Faith family doing?" he asked.

"They're fine. My 'family' is hanging in there," I said.

"That's great. I'm sure they think the world of you for giving them so much of yourself," he said. "I can't wait to meet them all."

"That day is coming," I told him. "And thank you for understanding my love for them."

"No problem. No problem at all."

After we talked a little while longer, I crawled into bed. The Faith's home was very nice, but I realized then that nothing could truly compare to home. That night, I slept like a baby. I was extremely happy that I did because I had an early rise for work the next morning.

After work, that next Tuesday evening, I called Zera. I just wanted to know that life was starting to settle well after the funeral and Aeria's admission to the mental trauma facility. Max had secured plane tickets for his wife and children to come visit him at the Faith manor. His intent was to propose to her and the kids a new life there in town with him as a reunited family. As far as Aeria was concerned, tests had already started. Initial results indicated that the potential for recovery looked very good! Zera had decided that she was not coming back to the city. She took it upon herself to make sure that the family business would continue to thrive as necessary. She also told me that life was about to drastically change for her. A lot of work was coming for her in the future; yet, she welcomed the challenge. She vowed to pray hard and maintain faith of steel. She knew that God would help her to do her very best.

§ § §

The Faithful Siblings

Maximus...

Max, of course, remained a very successful man, but he left his powerful corporate job in the big city. He took on the duty of helping Zera turn their father's small company into Faith Industries, as it is known today! Using his legal expertise and sharp savviness in the corporate arena, he armed Zera with the strategic prowess to move Faith Industries beyond their father's dreams. As he did so, he knew that Mr. Faith and God smiled down on him from the heavens above. He became one of the top community leaders in the town. Max strove to successfully grow the town's economy on a regional level. While he gained new allies and peers throughout his business dealings, he focused only on treasuring his relationships, opposed to abusing them for his own personal gain. No longer did he need to apologize to his mother and sisters for all of the disappointment, pain, and sorrow he put them through due to his previous abandonment of them. He had become extremely grateful that they never did the same to him, and he tended to their every need regardless of when they called upon him for assistance. Max continued to hold Zera's faith in highest regards because he knew that it helped him find his way and his purpose. On Zera's faith, Max grew to become an active member in the church, operating under the mentorship of Pastor Gabriel. Max flourished as a deacon, and he welcomed the opportunity to fulfill his father's roles as president of the trustee board and chairman of the charitable and for-profit affairs. Max was still a very busy man, but his family never suffered for it. His wife admired his determination to build the family empire while making sure he made it back for dinner nearly every night of the week. Max's children became fonder of him every day as he gave them the attention that they needed to mature through adolescence to adulthood.

Eventually, Max announced that his higher calling from the Lord was to preach! Ever dedicated to live the best life that he could in the name of God, he went back to college to receive all of the necessary theological credentials he needed to become a pastor. However, Max's fire to push himself as hard as he could never subsided; so he took another step further to obtain a doctorate degree in theological studies. Pastor Gabriel passed on to Glory, and since Max had done such a fantastic job serving as assistant pastor, he unanimously won the vote to be installed as Reverend Doctor Maximus Faith at New Beginnings Church of Christ.

Aeria...

After her release from the medical facility for mental trauma patients, Aeria never forgot about the long and difficult year that it took to recover. Once she recovered, she adjusted to home life and became a brand new wife, mother, and woman with a fresh take on life! She took pride in knowing that her kids and her husband depended on her wellbeing and her tender touch each and every day. Family visits to the Faith estate became quite frequent; and obviously, Momma Faith was pleased with that change in behavior. However, what really came as a shock to everyone was the weekend visit when Aeria attended church service and joined New Beginnings Church of Christ as a member! She testified right there after Dr. Faith's sermon—with the entire congregation as her witness—that God changed her life! She told everyone about how her father came to her in a vision after his death. She spoke of how he told her what she had to do in the name of Jesus to bring solid hope and fulfillment into her life.

"I learned from the error of my ways!" she shouted. "I learned from all my pain! It's all on me. I've got to know Jesus for myself! For no earthly things or experiences could ever fill a void created by the denial of God's awesome love and power in my soul! Amen!"

Soon after that testimony, Aeria and her husband moved to her hometown as well. They decided to build a grand mansion only minutes away from the Faith family estate. Shortly after that, their son and daughter were off to college to embark on their plans for bright and successful futures.

But the good news did not stop there. Aeria became an extremely hard-working woman. She dedicated herself to living up to her family name and traditions, despite the fact that she had spent her younger years running away from responsibility. She initially shocked the entire family when she excelled at the becoming the marketing director for the family business—working late nights while, tapping into new and lucrative industries for the company. That became normal protocol for Aeria. She remained the loving wife that Derrick profoundly loved. They grew to love each other so much that they did not think it was possible for anyone else to have a love quite like theirs.

Derrick also became immensely involved in the family business. He assumed the role of chief financial officer of Faith Industries. He took on that responsibility when it became too much for Maximus to handle, given his obligations to the church as pastor and overseer of all of its foundations, ministries, and business affairs. Thus, Derrick made sure that Faith Industries operated with utmost integrity, while retaining its path to rival any Fortune 500 company within the next five years.

Zera...

Zera became CEO of Faith Industries as well as a sought-after keynote speaker, far from the shy young woman that she once was. She became famous for her dedication to faith-based corporate success because she was not afraid to share her thoughts on keeping God involved in business! Zera even managed to find time to write a few bestselling books about this passion of hers. Thus, she traveled the world to spread her message far and wide. Zera had a miraculous gift for blending everyday subjects with corporate themes and God's omnipotent grace. Obviously, the role of CEO of Faith Industries was never an easy one for her to fulfill, but she never lost faith. With the family's blessings and the knowledge that her father was with her every step of the way, she always knew that she would not falter. In fact, her abundant life uncovered a new dimension of her faith, and Zera completely engulfed herself in it while she pushed the corporation forward to its incredibly bright future.

In her down time, Zera primarily relaxed at the Faith Manor. She remained forever proud of this home, the house her father built. She eventually renovated it to exude a spectacular Moroccan theme because she knew it would please Momma Faith to live out the rest of her days in a such a palatial space of serenity. Yet, recently, when Zera got time to travel for leisure, she started vacating to a newly built getaway house on the coast of Florida. Nevertheless, I knew that would never be home for her. The Faith manor was where her heart resided.

Beautiful, sun-drenched Florida could only provide to her temporary moments of peace and quiet.

Me...

One of Zera's speaking engagements brought her right here to the city, and I was delighted to receive a call from her personal assistant. Zera sent to us—my husband and me—front row tickets and VIP passes for the event. When we attended, we were both stunned and excited about the fact that the opera house was completely filled. I only knew her as my dear friend and God-sent sister, Zera; but there she was offering me a center stage view of God's wondrous power to change lives! That evening, she spoke on the topic of "God's Promises to His Children and Their Service in His Holy Name." As she delivered her message, the audience listened, shouted, received deliverance, and praised God to the highest! When she ended her ministry, she talked about our dearly departed Momma Faith. Zera, Aeria, Max, and I all missed her so much, but I was happy to witness Zera's profound commitment to changing people's lives as she spoke about the bittersweet happening:

> *"I was on travel when my mother died. I was speaking at another event. And before that event, I had just spoken to Momma. Everything was okay at that time. When I wrapped up my speaking engagement and went back to my hotel that night, I was tired. I closed my eyes, and I fell fast asleep. So that is when she came to me! She came to me in a vision, and she told*

me…on that night…that God had called her home! Oh, glory! She said she was happy to have spoken with my daddy too! She looked at me and told me she knew we were amazed at all that she did over the span of her life. She said, 'I know you, Zera, wondered how I was able to be so strong for you children and your Daddy while there was so much going on with the family business, finances, and struggles to become successful, while helping our friends and neighbors.' But you know what else she told me? She said that the Holy Spirit had never left her in the dark. She knew everything would be alright! Thank you, Lord! She told me that the higher power of faith—unbreakable faith—was her calling too! And she knew that she had passed on a beautiful gift to me that I would take to another level! Daddy came to me too. He held Momma's hand, and as they smiled. He said, 'Sweet child of God, spread your wings and your faith beyond the horizons. Let the masses grow and be strong from your favor! You are God's Daughter of Faith!' And that, my friends, is why I am here for you all tonight!"

The standing ovation was amazing! The crowd roared relentlessly, and the hearts of many changed on that very night. I felt it. When we went backstage to meet Zera, we thanked her for the amazing time we had during her ministry. I told her that I was proud of her. She gave me a huge hug, and she said, "Sister, you don't know how much that means to me."

We reveled in gratitude for our friendship and sisterhood. And then it came of no surprise to me—Zera's invitation to take us to dinner. I smile and said, "Sure, let's grab a bite and catch up!"

My husband decided to let us women catch up; and thus, Zera and I took her limousine to the best restaurant in the city, where we dined, laughed, and discussed our latest life adventures. Afterwards, Zera told her limousine driver to take an excursion to my home so that my husband would not have to make another trip to pick me up.

Before I got out of the limousine, Zera said, "Hold on. I want to give you something, but promise me you won't open it until you get in your house."

"Oh, Zera, no more," I said. "You've already done enough."

"God's blessings are meant to be shared," she returned. "Just promise me," she repeated.

"I promise," I said as Zera handed me a little black box with an envelope attached.

When I got in my home, I kissed my husband. Then I relaxed and took a shower. I thought about the wonderful message that Zera offered to everyone in the venue that night. I then grabbed the envelope and happily peeled it open. I knew the surprise was going to be something special, but I was not prepared for what would come next. Here is what that letter read:

Dear Sister and Faith Family Adopted Daughter in Love:

Momma and Daddy always loved you as their own. We siblings all feel the same. You're our sister! And now you have a wonderful husband to share with us as our new brother in Christ! So it should come as no surprise to you that we want to show our gratitude for your participation in our lives.

I am so sorry, Sis, that I missed your wedding. But I remember how much you loved that house when you called me and thanked me for letting you use it as your wedding venue. I barely have time these days to vacate, but I can assure you that I know just how peaceful, beautiful, and tranquil it is. Do you remember how you mentioned to me in an email that you hope that God blesses you with one just like it one day? Do you remember how much you told me that you loved Florida and the Fort Lauderdale coast? It was your third time there, and you called and told me that you could picture yourself being there forever. Well, Sis, the Lord has blessed you! And that house has always been meant for you. We just needed to make sure that all the legal aspects were in place. So open that little black box. In it you will find the key. And not only will you find that key, but also a key to a shiny new car and a Winnebago motorhome! At your earliest convenience go and meet Max and Aeria. They are all prepared to take care of you. It was very difficult for Aeria to keep all of these good blessings to herself. It's time for her to finally relax! She just knew she would ruin this surprise for you.

Love, Zera!

P.S. When you pick up your car, drive to the town bank. There will be a bankbook for you too, compliments of Momma and Daddy.

My hands were shaking as I finished reading that letter. My throat tightened with excitement, and tears drowned my eyes. I woke up my husband. I needed to share this great news with him. We laughed and cried together all through the rest of the night.

The next morning, we drove to the Faith family manor. When we arrived, we saw a beautiful coffee bean colored Porsche in the front courtyard along with a matching Winnebago Motor Home. Aeria and her husband came outside to greet me, and as I got out of the car, I nearly fell to ground because my knees were too weak to support me.

"Zera told me that when you arrive, I better see to it that you and your husband were okay!" she said with a chuckle.

I threw my hands up in the air, and cried tears of pure joy, praising God as loudly as I could. I then hugged everyone around me. Aeria's husband jumped in the new car to take a ride with my husband.

However, I went inside of the house with Aeria to get Zera on the phone. As Zera answered our phone call, she overflowed with laughter.

"Praise the Lord. Oh, praise the Lord!" she said. "See how amazing He truly is!"

"My Lord, yes, Zera!" I shouted. "Oh yes, I surely do! Words cannot express what I feel right now," I spoke as my voice cracked.

"Sometimes words are useless for what the heart truly feels," Zera responded.

Max then walked in the house and said, "God is so good, Isn't he!"

"Amen!" we all said.

"Amen," I repeated as the last lone voice.

§ § §

by Mrs. Patsy Bazile

The Faithful Conclusion

Dear reader, I know that it only takes one person to have faith. I know one person can have faith to move mountains just as the Bible tells us! If there is a need to make a change in your life, cry out to the Lord. Ask Him for the help that you need, for He is able to do the impossible. God will make a way out of no way. He has a plan for you, so do not give in to temptation. Refute the devil and his tempting schemes! Always remember that you are a masterpiece, made in the image of the Lord! You are designed by the Almighty Craftsman over all!

Metaphors of FAITH

WORDS OF A PRAYING WOMAN

by Mrs. Patsy Bazile

www.ingramcontent.com/pod-product-compliance
Lightning Source LLC
Chambersburg PA
CBHW051755040426
42446CB00007B/378